MW00835068

Hiking
the Allegheny
National Forest

Hiking
the Allegheny
National Forest

Exploring the Wilderness of
Northwestern Pennsylvania

Jeff Mitchell

STACKPOLE
BOOKS

Published by
STACKPOLE BOOKS
5067 Ritter Road
Mechanicsburg, PA 17055
www.stackpolebooks.com

Printed in the United States of America

10 9 8 7 6 5 4 3 2 1

FIRST EDITION

Cover design by Caroline Stover

Cover photo: Steve Davis and Ashley Lenig at Minister Creek. Photo by the author.

Hiking and backpacking are inherently risky activities with ever-changing conditions and numerous natural and man-made hazards. Many trails in this guide have dangerous natural conditions demanding respect and experience. All persons using the trails in this guide do so at their own risk. This guide is not a substitute for common sense, caution, and taking necessary safety precautions. The author and publisher disclaim any and all liability for conditions along the trails and routes of the included hikes, occurrences along them, and the accuracy of the data, conditions, and information contained herein.

Library of Congress Cataloging-in-Publication Data

Mitchell, Jeff.
    Hiking the Allegheny National Forest : exploring the wilderness of northwestern Pennsylvania / Jeff Mitchell.
        p.   cm.
    ISBN-13: 978-0-8117-3372-4 (pbk.)
    ISBN-10: 0-8117-3372-6 (paperback)
    1. Hiking–Pennsylvania–Allegheny National Forest–Guidebooks.
2. Allegheny National Forest (Pa.)–Guidebooks. I. Title.
GV199.42.P42A446   2007
796.5109748′9–dc22
                                                                2006018569

To Kaitlyn and Christian

Contents

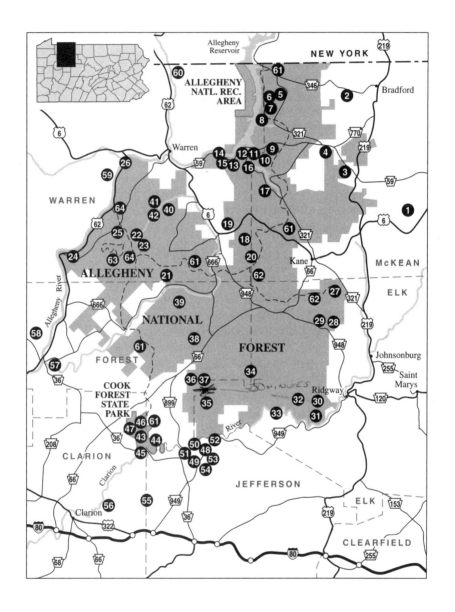

Preface

While growing up in northeastern Pennsylvania, I never had the opportunity to visit the Allegheny National Forest; the farthest west my family went was to Raystown Lake for camping and fishing trips. It wasn't until I attended law school at the University of Akron in Ohio that I finally had the opportunity to visit this beautiful region. During a weekend trip, I visited Tidioute Overlook, Minister Creek, Hearts Content, Kinzua Dam, Jakes Rocks, and Rimrock Overlook, and I was impressed by what I saw.

Several years passed, and I returned to my hometown of Tunkhannock. A friend lived outside Warren and worked for the Allegheny National Fish Hatchery. Whenever I went to visit, I drove along Route 6 to PA 59 at Smethport. I would then take PA 59 west into the national forest, passing the North Country and Morrison Trails, and the road to Rimrock Overlook. PA 59 descends to the Allegheny Reservoir, going by massive boulders along Wolf Run. I'd often stop at Kinzua Point to view the deep blue Allegheny Reservoir as it stretched off into the distance, contained by towering plateaus. From there, PA 59 hugs the side of the mountain as the reservoir narrows into a precipitous gorge, held by the impressive Kinzua Dam. Fishermen and canoeists were often below the dam, while schools of languid carp swam behind it, oblivious to everything except the bread crumbs people tossed down to them.

This was the best part of the ride, and it made the preceding three hours worthwhile. If the Allegheny National Forest looks this good from the road, I thought, imagine what it must look like from the trail. And the inspiration for this book was born.

I hope you enjoy this beautiful region as much as I have.

Thanks to all my friends and family, including Bryan Mulvihill, Bob Holliday, Jeff Sensenig, Ed Shrimp, Matt LaRusso, Dan Wrona, Carissa Longo, Chuck Pirone, and Paul and Paula Litwin.

This book would not be possible without the support of Kyle Weaver and Amy Cooper at Stackpole Books. I also thank all the volunteers who help maintain the trails in this book.

Finally, I owe a debt of gratitude to Ashley Lenig and Steve Davis for their help, hospitality, and friendship.

Introduction

This guide describes day hikes and backpacking trails in the Allegheny National Forest; Clear Creek, Cook Forest, Chapman, and Kinzua Bridge State Parks; Cornplanter and Clear Creek State Forests; and various state game and watershed lands. Descriptions of each trail's length, difficulty, terrain, highlights, elevation change, and trailhead directions are provided. Although this region of Pennsylvania is not as rugged as others, the hikes in this guide vary greatly in length and difficulty. The majority follow established trails, but there are a few bushwhacks.

With the growing popularity of the North Country Trail, the Allegheny National Forest region continues to attract an increasing number of hikers and backpackers from the Midwest, Northeast, and Mid-Atlantic. As this guide illustrates, the national forest region is a hiking wonderland, offering many different trails with varied scenery and habitats. Here you will find beautiful rivers and streams, scenic valleys and gorges, excellent camping, expansive vistas, old-growth forest, and imposing rock formations, boulders, and outcrops. Despite being a day's drive from some of the most heavily populated areas in the country, the Allegheny National Forest provides surprising isolation and solace, and some of the most scenic hiking in Pennsylvania.

History

By the early twentieth century, most of the eastern United States was devoid of old-growth forest as a result of careless logging practices. The federal government became aware that such mindless exploitation caused great damage to watersheds, habitats, and wildlife. As a result, Congress passed the Weeks Act in 1911, allowing the federal government to buy lands in eastern states for national forests. The Allegheny National Forest (ANF) was created in 1923. These forests would have a multiuse concept, meaning they would provide a multitude of services, including logging, watershed protection, recreation, wilderness, open space, mineral extraction, and habitat for wildlife. This concept governs our national forests to this day and is essential to understanding the various interests they must support.

Terrain and Geology

Like most of Pennsylvania, the ANF is dominated by plateaus ranging between 1,600 and 2,300 feet in elevation. These plateaus are heavily dissected by streams, creeks, runs, and rivers creating numerous glens, gorges, and valleys. Many slopes of these plateaus are steep, particularly along the Allegheny Reservoir.

A dominant geologic feature of the forest is the prevalence of rock formations: large boulders, rock cities, ledges, and outcrops. They are made up of resistant sedimentary and conglomerate rocks that once formed the cap on top of the plateaus, and still do. These rock formations are often found along the edges and slopes of the plateau and in stream or river valleys, and many have tectonic caves. Unlike limestone caves, where water has dissolved the limestone to create the cave, tectonic caves are formed by the movement and separation of rocks and boulders. Most of the caves in the ANF are not even a few hundred feet in length.

The greatest elevations are located in the northern section of the forest. The southern half features lower elevations and more moderate terrain.

Forests

Before human intervention, the ANF primarily consisted of beech, hemlock, sugar maple, birch, white pine, and chestnut trees, with black cherry constituting less than 1 percent. Today, however, the forest is dominated by black cherry, red maple, and other hardwoods. Hemlocks and white pines are mostly found along streams. The forest's understory is often composed of mountain laurel, lowbush blueberry, brush, ferns, and rhododendrons along some streams and rivers. One of the largest remaining old-growth forests in the eastern United States lies within the Tionesta National Scenic and Research Natural Areas.

Rivers and Streams

The ANF has more than 800 miles of rivers and streams, making it an ideal place for fishing and canoeing. Many of these streams are known for their beauty and water quality. The three rivers that dominate the ANF are the Allegheny River, Tionesta Creek, and Clarion River.

Quick facts about the ANF

- Covers over 513,000 acres
- Contains 201 miles of hiking trails, 53 miles of cross-country ski trails, and 18 miles of interpretive trails
- Features two wilderness areas, Hickory Creek and Allegheny River Islands; the Allegheny National Recreation Area; Hearts Content and Tionesta National Scenic Areas; and the Tionesta National Research Area
- Includes the Allegheny Reservoir, with 90 miles of shoreline and covering 12,080 acres at summer pool
- Is home to two national wild and scenic rivers, the Allegheny and Clarion
- Is crossed by a 90-mile segment of the North Country National Scenic Trail, which will eventually stretch from North Dakota to New York
- Is visited by approximately 2 million people annually
- Lies within a day's drive of half the nation's population
- Besides hiking and backpacking, offers extensive opportunities for hunting, fishing, camping, canoeing, wildlife-watching, ATVs, mountain biking, scenic driving, snowmobiles, cross-country skiing, snowshoeing, and rock and ice climbing

The Allegheny River is a large, scenic river that flows along the northern and western boundaries of the ANF. This river drains the entire forest, and portions of it are designated as a national wild and scenic river. In 1965, the Kinzua Dam was built across the river to form the Allegheny Reservoir, a flood control project. The most incredible scenery is the canyon between Kinzua Dam and Warren, with deep pools, large boulders, and several islands. Popular species of fish are walleye, smallmouth bass, pickerel, muskellunge, and trout. The river also contains the Allegheny River Islands Wilderness, a group of seven islands that feature old-growth forest, historic sites, and great campsites. Not surprisingly, the Allegheny is a popular canoe river.

The Tionesta Creek drains the heart of the ANF and joins the Allegheny River at Tionesta. This large stream can also be characterized as a small river and contains riffles, pools, and boulders. It is home to smallmouth bass and trout. Whereas the Allegheny and Clarion Rivers are more popular, the Tionesta offers isolation as it flows through the wilderness. Its banks are not as developed with summer homes as the Allegheny's and the stream is smaller than the Clarion. With less development, camping opportunities abound, and canoeists are increasingly exploring the Tionesta.

The Clarion River, another national wild and scenic river, is truly in a class by itself. The Clarion offers fine water quality, superb campsites, good fishing, isolation, and excellent scenery. These attributes make it one of Pennsylvania's most popular rivers, and it attracts canoeists from across the eastern United States. This river forms the southern boundary of the ANF between Ridgway and Clear Creek State Park. The section between Ridgway and Irwin Run takeout offers the best scenery, isolation, and campsites.

Wildlife

The ANF is home to 315 species of animals. Hunted species, such as deer, wild turkey, and bear, are common. River otters were reintroduced in 1991 and fishers in 1997. Five threatened or endangered species live in the forest, including the Bald Eagle, two types of mussels, the Indiana Bat, and an orchid. There are at least 71 fish species in the forest.

Issues Facing the ANF

Over the past few years, there has been growing attention to the management of our national forests. As with most national forests, several environmental issues face the ANF that have garnered significant local attention and discussion.

The ANF, like all national forests, exists for multiuse purposes. Many people, however, feel there has been an overemphasis on economic interests within the forest at the expense of wilderness, outdoor recreation, and environmental conservation and preservation. The two primary economic interests are logging and mineral extraction in the form of drilling for oil and natural gas. These instrumental activities have brought economic opportunity to the region and provide employment for local residents. These economic interests, however, must also be balanced with environmental concerns.

Forest Management and Biodiversity

The ANF is world renowned for its valuable black cherry. This tree, however, has been promoted throughout the forest because of its cash value. This has resulted in a loss of the forest's biodiversity. Before the

ANF was logged, black cherry accounted for less than 1 percent of all trees; now it represents a third of all trees in the forest. Over the same time period, there has been a significant decline in the percentages of beech, hemlock, sugar maple, and white pine. Approximately 90 percent of the entire forest is open to logging. The forest's biodiversity is also threatened by acid rain from the industrialized Ohio River valley.

Oil and Natural Gas

Deposits of oil and natural gas underlie most of the ANF. The federal government owns the mineral rights under only about 7 percent of the forest; most mineral rights are in private hands. Thousands of oil and gas wells, and their attendant machinery, dot the forest; they are a common sight along many trails. The ANF is the most heavily drilled national forest in the country, with approximately 7,000 active oil and gas wells. In fact, the ANF may have more oil and gas wells than all other national forests combined. The roads, wells, pipelines, and electric lines for oil and gas production cover 50,000 acres of the ANF.

Roads

The ANF contains more than 4,000 miles of roads, including federal, state, township, forest, and oil and gas roads. Such an extensive system of roads compromises the forest's scenic and wilderness values. Many feel that roadless areas in the forest should be expanded and unused roads should be seeded and returned to natural habitat. But because 93 percent of mineral rights are privately owned, the forest cannot prevent the construction of roads to access oil and gas deposits, and many of the roads in the forest are for oil and gas wells. Another reason why the ANF has so many roads is that prior to its creation, there were many roads to access lumber camps and towns. Unlike other national forests, the ANF was not an untouched wilderness when it was created in 1923.

Wilderness

There has also been a growing movement to expand the acreage of wilderness and protected areas in the ANF. Presently, the forest is home to only two wilderness areas: Hickory Creek and Allegheny Islands. These wilderness areas cover less than 2 percent of the forest, one of the lowest percentages of any national forest. There is precedent for expanding the ANF's wilderness areas: In 1973, Senators Scott and Schweiker supported expanding wilderness in the forest. Unfortunately, the House of Representatives failed to pass the amendments. It is hoped that proposals to expand the wilderness in the ANF will become a reality.

Hiking Trails

The ANF has a limited system of hiking trails, considering its size and popularity, with about 200 miles. In comparison, the Monongahela National Forest has 500 miles of trails, and the White Mountain National Forest has 1,000 miles. The ANF and the North Country Trail continue to grow in popularity, drawing hikers from across the East and Midwest. Hiking is very popular in the forest, involving more than 50 percent of all visitors to the ANF. With such a limited trail system, several trails, such as Minister Creek, Hickory Creek, Morrison, and sections of the Tracy Ridge Hiking Trail System, are showing signs of overuse. Just as the ANF has recognized the popularity of ATV and snowmobile use by greatly expanding those trail systems, it should also consider the expansion of hiking and backpacking trails.

Trailblazing is also problematic in the forest. Most trails are blazed by gray, white, or blue diamond-shaped placards nailed to trees. These placards require maintenance and are costly. The white or gray blazes often blend in with the trunks of hardwood trees, making them harder to notice, and the placards frequently fall from the trees. As a result, some trails may be hard to follow. Instead, it would be better if standard paint blazes were used.

The North Country National Scenic Trail is the longest and most famous trail in the forest, attracting hikers from across the country. Despite its renown and status, the trail does not have a buffer, and forest roads, wells, pipelines, and other development are common along the trail corridor. The ANF should permit trail relocations in undisturbed and scenic locations away from such development and protect the trail with a buffer.

Another hiking issue is the lack of a long-distance loop trail system in the forest. Most loop trails, such as Morrison, Minister Creek, and Hickory Creek, are short and can be hiked in a day. Longer loops, similar to the Quehanna, Black Forest, Chuck Keiper, and Susquehannock Trails found in north-central Pennsylvania, should be constructed in the forest. Most of the forest's trail system is linear, making it less attractive for hikers, who must shuttle cars and make prior arrangements. A more cohesive trail system also would benefit other users, such as hunters or fishermen. Hunters in particular use hiking trails heavily to access the forest.

Day-hiking loops within the forest are surprisingly limited; many hikes in this guide are fairly short. Furthermore, some of the most scenic areas in the forest do not have official trails. For example, the Hickory Creek Trail never meets its beautiful namesake. Nor are there official trails that explore the Clarion River Rapids, Logan Falls, Pigeon Run Falls, Hector Falls, or East Branch Tionesta Creek. Millstone, Spring, and Bear Creeks in the southern part of the forest feature magnificent scenery and isolation, yet there are no trails.

I make the following recommendations to enhance the ANF's trail system. Most of these recommendations are in management areas where outdoor recreation is emphasized. Furthermore, several of these trail recommendations would follow established grade or old forest roads, making construction more convenient and less costly.

- The Tracy Ridge Hiking Trail System is extensive but does not showcase some of the most scenic areas, which are the reservoir and streams. For example, there aren't any true vistas as indicated on the map. Construct trails along the ridge between Tracy Ridge Campground and the North Country Trail above Willow Bay, where there are rock outcrops; along Tracy Run and North Branch; along the reservoir between Polly's Run and Nelse Run; and along Nelse Run north toward Tracy Ridge Campground.
- Create an excellent loop with the Tracy Ridge Hiking Trail System by constructing a trail from the North Country Trail along North Branch Sugar Run, turning north and ascending Indian Run, and then turning west and ending at PA 321, near the Tracy Ridge Campground.
- Build two connector trails between the Morrison Trail and the North Country Trail along Hemlock Run; one at the northern end of the loop and the other at the southern end along the reservoir. Construct trails to connect Rimrock Overlook and Kinzua Beach to the Morrison Trail.
- Construct a 4- to 7-mile loop trail in the Tionesta National Scenic and Research Areas to showcase the incredible old-growth forests. The trail that presently exists is very limited.
- Build a 15- to 20-mile loop trail along the Clarion River by incorporating the southern half of the Laurel Mill Trail and constructing a connector trail along scenic Bear Creek.

- Create a 3- to 4-mile loop trail along the oxbow loop of the Clarion River near Irwin Run to showcase the impressive scenery of the Clarion River Rapids.
- Enhance the scenery and length of the Hickory Creek Trail, one of the most popular in the forest, by following the old railroad grades along the beautiful Middle and East Hickory Creeks.
- Expand the trails beyond the Tanbark Trail in the Allegheny National Recreation Area to include scenic mountain streams and rock outcrops by building loop or linear trails.

The ANF's trail system needs to be assessed and evaluated based on increasing usage and the various interests and needs of those visitors who hike and backpack.

Balancing the Interests

As you can see, these issues are complex. A balance must be struck between the various interests that rely on the forest. Proposals to ban commercial logging or oil and natural gas extraction are not realistic. On the other hand, the forest is not purely a moneymaking enterprise; it must also provide opportunities for outdoor enthusiasts and protect watersheds, wilderness, wildlife, and habitats. By carefully managing the forest's economic resources, ecologic and scenic values, and outdoor recreational opportunities, we all will benefit.

Howard Zahniser

Howard Zahniser was born in 1906 in Franklin, Pennsylvania, and spent much of his childhood in Tionesta. He became executive director of the Wilderness Society and was also the author of the National Wilderness Preservation System Act of 1964, commonly called the Wilderness Act of 1964. It was through this act that more than 100 million acres of wilderness have received protection. This act is also notable because it gave wilderness federal protection and placed natural preservation as a priority over human use, development, and exploitation.

Howard Zahniser died in 1964, four months before the Wilderness Act was signed into law by President Lyndon Johnson. He is buried in Tionesta. Zahniser is widely respected as one of Pennsylvania's premier conservationists; the words he wrote more than forty years ago continue to be the gold standard today: "A wilderness . . . is hereby recognized as an area where the earth and its community of life are untrammeled by man, where man himself is a visitor who does not remain."

Chief Cornplanter

Chief Cornplanter was a famous and respected leader of the Seneca Indians. He continues to be a well-known figure today, with many places named after him, including the Cornplanter State Forest.

Cornplanter was born around 1742 to a Seneca mother and a Dutch father. During the Revolutionary War, he supported the British, but he later supported peace and cooperation with the Americans. Cornplanter attempted to address the grievances of his people through negotiation, accepted the use of modern technology by his people, and supported the integration of the Senecas into the local economies. To a limited degree, Cornplanter believed his people should learn the modern ways of American society so that they could better preserve their traditions and culture. This position would create a rift between himself, his political rivals, and his half-brother, Handsome Lake.

Thanks to his cooperation and negotiation with the Americans, Cornplanter was able to establish a land base within the ancestral territory of the Senecas. The Seneca Indian Reservation exists today across the border in New York. The 1,500-acre Cornplanter Land Grant is in Pennsylvania, although most of it is now under the Allegheny Reservoir. The preservation of this land for his people would be regarded as Cornplanter's greatest accomplishment.

It is believed that Chief Cornplanter often visited a cave in the northern part of the ANF, near the Allegheny River. The location of this almost mythical cave has never been determined, and people continue to look for it. Chief Cornplanter died in 1835.

Clubs and Organizations

The following clubs and organizations are active in the ANF region by organizing trips, maintaining trails, or both. Consider supporting them to enjoy and preserve the ANF region's hiking trails.

- Sierra Club, Allegheny Group, PO Box 8241, Pittsburgh, PA 15217; phone: 412-802-6161; website: www.alleghenysc.org; e-mail: info@alleghenysc.org
- Sierra Club, Lake Erie Group, PO Box 1556, Erie, PA 16507-0556
- Butler Outdoor Club, PO Box 243, Butler, PA 16003-0243; website: www.butleroutdoorclub.org
- North Country Trail Assocation, 229 East Main Street, Lowell, MI 49331; phone: 888-454-6282; website: www.northcountrytrail.org; e-mail: HQ@northcountrytrail.org

- ANF Chapter of the North Country Trail Association, website: www.northcountrytrail.org/anf/index/htm; e-mail: anfchapter @northcountryail.org
- Harmony Trails Council, PO Box 243, Ingomar, PA 18127; websites: www.harmonytrails.com and www.rachelcarsontrail.com
- Keystone Trails Association, PO Box 129, Confluence, PA 15424; phone: 814-395-9696; website: www.kta-hike.org; e-mail: info@ kta-hike.org

Camping Regulations

Backcountry camping is liberally permitted along trails within the forest, except within 1,500 feet of the tree line along the Allegheny Reservoir, day-use areas, within 200 feet of a road, and in national scenic or research areas.

Cross-Country Skiing Trails

The ANF contains several cross-country skiing trails that are included in this guide. Hiking is permitted on these trails; however, keep in mind that they usually are not as well blazed or established as other trails. Cross-country skiing trails are generally wider and have bridges over almost all stream crossings. These trails offer great snowshoeing. If hiking or snowshoeing in winter, please do not walk in the cross-country ski tracks.

Hiking and Backpacking during Hunting Season

The ANF is a popular hunting destination, and every trail in this guide passes through public land open to hunting. During hunting season, make sure to wear fluorescent orange while hiking, as recommended by the Pennsylvania Game Commission, and be considerate of hunters. Wearing fluorescent orange is required on state game lands. Hunting is not permitted on Sundays. Try not to disturb a hunt or wildlife. It is important for hikers to be respectful of other outdoor users. For more information about hunting seasons, visit www.pgc.state.pa.us.

Trailhead Parking

Many trailheads are located in isolated areas, and vandalism of vehicles does occasionally occur. To protect your vehicle, make sure it is locked, all windows are closed, and anything of value is placed out of sight. Commonsense precautions will go a long way to protect your vehicle.

Maps

It is very important to have a map and, if one is available, a guide for any trail you plan to backpack. Maps of most Allegheny National Forest trails are free; these maps also often have descriptions and directions to the trail. For a free map, contact the ranger district where the trail is located or the forest's headquarters. All state parks provide free quality maps with directions and information about the park. State forests also furnish free maps. Guides and maps for the North Country and Baker Trails are available for a price. Maps for all state game lands can be purchased for a few dollars or downloaded for free from www.pgc.state.pa.us.

Individual maps of each hike are included throughout this guide. Below is a legend for the specific features found on the maps.

Map Legend			
	Rapids	V	View, vista, overlook
	Waterfalls, cascades	⌂	House, cabin, other structure
	Creeks, streams, runs, brooks		Roads (dotted line indicates extremely rough road)
	Swamps, wetlands		Utility, power-line, pipeline swath
P	Parking area		
	Trail	o—o	Gate
	Other trail	⊼	Picnic area
	Blowdowns, thick brush along trail	△	Campground, campsite
	Cliffs, ledges, rock faces, boulders	)(	Bridge

Hiking and Backpacking Safety

It never ceases to amaze me how many people go hiking or backpacking without taking even minimal safety precautions to insure their safety. The following are important to ensure your safety:

- Water is absolutely critical, regardless of the difficulty or length of the trail. Always carry a water filter or other chemical treatment; all wilderness water sources should be treated.
- Take along sufficient food.
- Tell someone where you will be hiking or backpacking, and if you can, go with a friend.
- Wear proper footwear and dress appropriately for the weather and elevation. Synthetic materials and wool are recommended. When wet, cotton loses its insulation capacity and dries very slowly, creating a risk of hypothermia. Never hike or backpack in cold temperatures unless you have the proper equipment and experience.
- Obtain a map, learn how to read maps, and acquire as much information as possible about the trails you plan to backpack.
- Carry a flashlight and a small medical pack.
- Check the weather report before you leave.
- Be careful when hiking along or crossing streams and creeks in high water. Always unbuckle the hip belt of your backpack when crossing deep streams.
- Choose trails that are appropriate for your ability and experience.

Trail Registers

Some trails in this guide occasionally have trail registers. It is important to sign them for several reasons:

- Safety. If something were to happen to you on the trail, it would be easier to determine your location and direction if you had signed the register.
- Government assistance. It is easier to acquire grants and funding to preserve and maintain trails that are being used. The most accurate way to determine use is by the number of names in a register.
- Trail conditions and warnings. Previous hikers and backpackers often write trail conditions, warnings, and their experiences on the trail, which can be helpful to subsequent backpackers.
- Camaraderie. Registers create a sense of kinship and camaraderie on the trail.

Hiking and Backpacking Etiquette

Unfortunately, there are some people who show disrespect toward nature. Please note the following:

- Pack out everything you brought; if you can, pack out litter left by others.
- Do not pick any vegetation or disturb, harm, or feed any wildlife.
- Do not take shortcuts, particularly across switchbacks, which causes erosion.
- Do not deface, remove, carve into, or damage anything.
- Follow all rules and regulations established by the state parks, forests, game lands, or other controlling authority.
- When camping, follow leave-no-trace ethics

Respect Public Property

Most of the trails in this guide are on public property. Public land must be respected. Too many people feel they have the right to use, pollute, and exploit public land any way they see fit. Always follow regulations of public agencies regarding the use of public lands, and help pack out litter or clear dumpsites. We all need to be more appreciative of the public land that has been provided for our benefit.

Bears

The black bear calls the ANF home and can be found along all the trails in this guide. For the experienced hiker, seeing a bear is a highlight of a trip, because these shy, retiring creatures usually avoid human interaction. For the beginning backpacker, no other animal causes more stress or worry.

Black bears do not need to be feared; they need to be treated with intelligence and respect. You should always avoid cubs and keep your distance from them, because their mother will be overprotective and more likely to be aggressive. Make noise when hiking through thick brush; surprising a bear can result in an attack. The sound of clapping or human voices is generally sufficient. Always rig your food in a tree, as well as soap, toothpaste, and utensils, and avoid cooking meat when camping. Never keep food in your tent, as a hungry bear will slice through it easily.

If you do find yourself faced with an aggressive bear, back away slowly, avoid eye contact, and wave and clap your hands to make yourself appear larger. If a bear does charge you, it will typically be a bluff. If a black bear attacks you, however, you must fight back. The tactic of playing dead applies to brown or grizzly bears, which do not live in Pennsylvania. For this reason, I typically hike with a trusty hiking stick. Hiking with a partner would further discourage a bear attack.

There is no need to be alarmed. In almost every case, a bear will leave the area where you are hiking without your ever knowing. Because bears are heavily hunted and not commonly fed in Pennsylvania, they do not pose the same problem or nuisance as those found in the Adirondacks or Shenandoah and Great Smoky Mountains National Parks. However, you must be prepared in the unlikely situation that you are confronted with an aggressive bear.

Snakes

Pennsylvania is home to three species of venomous snakes: timber rattlesnake, eastern copperhead, and the massasauga rattlesnake. Snakes are not as common along trails in the ANF as they are in other areas of the state. Your greatest chances of encountering them are in the rock cities throughout the forest.

The timber rattlesnake grows to 35 to 74 inches, is most active between April and October, and occurs in both the common black-brown phase and the rare yellow phase. This snake often enjoys sunning on rocks. Its habitat is throughout much of the state, but you are more likely to see it along trails in the north-central part of the state and along dry, rocky ridgetop trails.

The eastern copperhead grows to 22 to 53 inches and also enjoys sunning on rocks. It too lives throughout much of the state, but it tends to be more common along trails in the north-central region.

The massasauga rattlesnake grows to 18 to 39 inches and generally lives in swamps, bogs, wetlands, or rivers. This snake is very rare in Pennsylvania and lives only in the far western part of the state. It is highly unlikely you will ever see this snake.

Like bears, snakes tend to be shy creatures that are afraid of humans. Snake bites are rare and typically occur when people harass or even try to handle a snake. When you approach a snake, always give it a wide berth and observe it from a safe distance. Do not harm snakes, as they are becoming increasingly rare and may be protected by law. Most of my snake encounters have been along rocks exposed to the sun, so be mindful when hiking this type of terrain. Thankfully, rattlesnakes almost always let you know if you are getting too close with a shrill rattle.

If a snake does bite you, seek medical attention immediately. The venom of these snakes generally is not fatal to an adult but can kill a small child. Keep the wound clean, immobilized as best you can, and if possible, above your heart.

In all of my hiking trips, I have only seen poisonous snakes about seven times. These sightings are highlights of any trip. Because snakes are so crucial to our ecosystem, please respect them.

Stinging Nettles

Various species of nettles grow throughout the United States. In Pennsylvania, stinging nettles tend to grow in large groups or patches; they have heart-shaped leaves and are generally 1 to 3 feet in height but can reach 5 feet. The stems have fine needles that pierce the skin and deliver formic acid. The result is a red, itchy, burning rash that can cause welts and blisters. Fortunately, this annoyance is usually temporary and can be alleviated by water, saliva, baking powder, or any alkaline substance.

Stinging nettles are often found along the trails of north-central Pennsylvania but are somewhat less common in the ANF. These plants are most prevalent in summer months and grow in shaded, wet areas, such as along streams and glens. Your best defense is simply to wear long pants while hiking through these areas.

Lyme Disease

In Pennsylvania, Lyme disease is a bacterial infection transmitted by the bites of infected deer ticks. Very few tick bites actually lead to the disease. When a person is bitten by an infected deer tick, the disease develops in a few days to week, with a circular rash enveloping the bite and flulike symptoms. If caught early enough, the disease can be successfully treated with antibiotics.

The risk of infection increases when the tick is attached for thirty-six to forty-eight hours. Most people will find a full-grown tick within that time, so the greatest risk of infection comes from tiny ticks in the nymphal stage, which are about the size of a period.

Deer ticks are common in the woods, but they tend to prefer grassy and brushy areas. Some insect repellents are effective against ticks. Wear long pants and sleeves, and inspect your body for any ticks at the end of the day.

Giardiasis

There is no reason why any hiker should become infected with giardiasis or any other water-borne bacterial or microbial infection. Everyone should know that all water sources, even pristine springs, must be treated. With the advent of lightweight effective water filters and various chemical purifiers, it is convenient for any hiker to have safe water.

Giardiasis is significant because it wreaks havoc with the digestive and intestinal tract. Fortunately, it can be successfully treated with appropriate medical attention.

Hiking through Northwest Pennsylvania's Seasons

Winter

Winter is a surprisingly popular time to hike. There are no bugs, stifling heat, or crowds. Water sources also tend to be more prevalent, and the lack of leaves affords more views, enabling hikers to peer deep into the forest and observe features that at other times are concealed by foliage. The ANF region typically receives heavy snowfall, particularly lake-effect snowfalls, and most trails are ideal for snowshoeing. Snow cover presents a profusion of animal tracks, which always add interest to a hike. Do not attempt winter hiking unless you are experienced and have the proper equipment, including snowshoes or crampons.

Spring

With plentiful water, budding trees, and a profusion of wildflowers and wildlife, spring is an excellent time to backpack in northwestern Pennsylvania. Streams tend to be filled with water and are at their most impressive; however, fording these streams can be difficult and dangerous. Trail conditions are often wet and boggy. Spring in this part of the state tends to be temperate and wet; snow sometimes lingers into mid-April in higher elevations. Increasing daylight enables you to cover more miles and longer trails.

Summer

For many hikers, summer is the least favorite season to hike. Northwestern Pennsylvania often has hot and humid summers, and bugs are a nuisance. The good news is that most trails in this guide pass through mountain laurel, which blooms in late June through early

July, and rhododendron, which blooms in mid-July. The incredible blossoms are a highlight of any hike. Lowbush blueberries can also be found along some trails, and the berries ripen in July. The water sources diminish along some trails during this usually drier season.

Autumn

Autumn is probably the favorite season for hikers, with cool, crisp weather and more available water sources. The highlight is the incredible color changes in foliage that sweep through the expansive hardwood forests; in northwestern Pennsylvania, the change takes place from late September to late October. Hunting is very popular in the ANF, so it's important to be aware of hunting seasons and wear fluorescent orange.

Backpacking for Beginners

Many day hikers are interested in backpacking but feel intimidated about giving it a try. The transition is surprisingly easy. Follow these simple tips for your first trip:

- Choose a relatively short, easy trail offering a one-night trip.
- Acquire a map and learn everything about the trail you plan to backpack.
- Beginning backpackers are infamous for packing too heavily; concentrate on packing light and carrying only what you'll need. An unbearably heavy pack will ruin any trip. Pack dehydrated foods.
- Take along a friend familiar with backpacking.
- Purchase or rent the proper equipment. You'll need a pack at least 3,500 cubic inches in volume; a sleeping bag rated to at least 20 degrees Fahrenheit for three-season backpacking or a liner if backpacking in summer; a sleeping pad, especially important in cold temperatures; a tent; a water filter or chemical treatment; and hiking boots. This may sound like a lot of equipment, but it will last you a lifetime if you take care of it.
- Learn about leave-no-trace ethics, outdoor survival skills, and how to rig your food properly.
- A wealth of how-to guides are available for beginning backpackers. Also check the websites www.backpacker.com and www.thebackpacker.com for informative forums.

Hike Recommendations

The following sections give recommendations based on what you want to experience on your hike.

Hikes with Waterfalls or Cascades

- Hector Falls
- Bent Run Waterfalls
- Pigeon Run Falls
- Logan Falls
- Morrison Trail Loop

Hikes with Vistas

- Seneca Point and River Trail
- Minister Creek
- Rimrock Overlook
- Jakes Rocks
- Tidioute Overlook
- Beartown Rocks Trail

Hikes with Old-Growth Forest

- Anders Run Natural Area
- Forest Cathedral
- Cook Trail
- Seneca Point and River Trail
- Tionesta National Scenic Area
- Hearts Content National Scenic Area

Hikes with Rock Outcrops, Boulders, and Formations

- Minister Creek
- Morrison Trail Loop
- East Hickory Creek
- Hector Falls
- Rimrock Overlook
- Jakes Rocks
- Beartown Rocks Trail
- Seneca Point and River Trail
- Campbell Mill Loop Interpretive Trail

Hikes that Are Ideal for Wildlife-Watching

- Little Drummer Historical Pathway
- Buzzard Swamp Trail
- Beaver Meadows
- Akeley Swamp

Trails for Children

These trails are the easiest, most interesting, and most ideal for children. Even though they are easy and shorter than other trails in this guide, please understand they still contain natural hazardous conditions that require parental supervision and common sense.

- Kinzua Bridge
- Marilla Bridges Trail
- Timberdoodle Flats Interpretive Trail
- Rimrock Overlook
- Jakes Rocks
- Bent Run Waterfalls
- Little Boulder Nature Trail
- Smorgasbord Forest Trail
- Hearts Content National Scenic Area
- Buckaloons Seneca Interpretive Trail
- Akeley Swamp
- Tidioute Overlook
- Forest Cathedral
- Black Bear Trail
- Phyllis Run Trail
- Pigeon Run Falls
- Summit, Plantation, and Information Center Loop Trails

Most Scenic Trails

Everyone's preferences are different, and I usually do not list the most scenic trails. However, I think most people would agree that these trails and places are the most scenic and should not be missed.

Allegheny National Forest: Bradford Ranger District

- Tracy Ridge and Johnnycake Trails
- Allegheny Reservoir and Nelse Run
- Morrison Trail Loop

- Rimrock Overlook
- Jakes Rocks
- Bent Run Waterfalls
- Hector Falls
- Tionesta National Scenic Area
- Minister Creek
- Hearts Content National Scenic Area
- Tom's Run and Ironwood Loops
- East Hickory Creek

Allegheny National Forest: Marienville Ranger District

- Little Drummer Historical Pathway
- Clarion River Rapids
- Pigeon Run Falls
- Beaver Meadows
- Logan Falls

Cook Forest State Park

- Cook Trail
- Forest Cathedral
- Seneca Point and River Trail

Clear Creek State Park and State Forest

- Hunters and Irish Rock Trails
- Tadler Run Trail
- Clear Creek Trail
- Beartown Rocks Trail

State Game Lands 74

- Mill Creek Gorge

Cornplanter State Forest

- Anders Run Natural Area

Kinzua Bridge
State Park

This park was the home of the Kinzua Bridge, a 2,053-foot viaduct that is a national engineering landmark. When it was built in 1882, it was the highest and longest railroad bridge in the world. It was reconstructed in 1900 to accommodate heavier trains. The state park officially opened in 1970.

The viaduct has been a tourist attraction for over a century. Spanning the Kinzua Gorge against a backdrop of fall foliage, it was a sight to behold. Excursion trains from Kane began to take visitors across the bridge in 1987. These trips ended in 2002, however, when inspections revealed significant deterioration to the structure. Repairs began in February 2003.

Unfortunately, on July 21, 2003, the history of the park and its namesake were changed forever when a tornado struck the bridge. Eleven supporting towers collapsed; only nine were left standing. Because of the cost, there are no plans to rebuild the bridge. This park, once an impressive example of human ingenuity, is now a testament to the awesome power of nature.

1. Kinzua Bridge

Duration: 1/2 hour

Distance: .2 mile

Difficulty: Easy

Blazes: None

Terrain: Level and rolling, with gradual descents and ascents

Elevation change: 30 feet

Trail conditions: Trails follow paved walkways

Highlights: Views of the Kinzua Gorge, remnants of the Kinzua Bridge, the windblown forest

Directions: From Mount Jewett, follow SR 3011 north for 4 miles. From PA 59, just west of the intersection with PA 646, follow SR 3011 south for 6 miles.

From the parking area, follow the walkway down to the viewing platforms that overlook the remains of the bridge, gorge, and forest. The most incredible feature is the effect the tornado had on the forest.

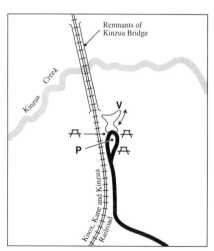

Hike 1: Kinzua Bridge

For as far as the eye can see to the east, the trees are uniformly blown down. It appears as if the tornado came from the east, which is odd, since most storms travel from west to east. It also appears as if the tornado hit the bridge and stopped or blew from the southwest, since the forest to the west of the bridge is largely intact. It is odd to view a bridge with its middle torn out. Most of the surviving towers are on the side of the gorge closest to the state park facilities.

The collapsed towers were pushed to the west and lie crumpled at the bottom of the gorge, where they will remain. A trail also went down to Kinzua Creek at the base of the bridge; it is now closed until cleanup is completed.

I never had the opportunity to see Kinzua Bridge before it was destroyed. I had seen pictures of the bridge with the latticework of its towers framing a background of beautiful fall foliage. Pictures are all we have now of this remnant from our past.

Bradford City
Water Authority

The Bradford City Water Authority owns 12,000 acres of watershed lands that are open to hunting, hiking, and fishing. These lands are located east of Tracy Ridge. Off-trail exploration will take you to impressive rock cities and caves. The authority maintains two trails: Marilla Bridges Trail and Indian Pipe Trail. Indian Pipe Trail is a 7-mile linear trail that follows a gated road and is probably of greater interest to mountain bikers or cross-country skiers than hikers. For contact information, visit www.bradfordwater.com.

🚶🚶 2. Marilla Bridges Trail

Duration: ½ hour

Distance: .8-mile loop

Difficulty: Easy

Blazes: None

Terrain: Level

Elevation change: 20 feet

Trail conditions: Trail is wide, level, and well established

Highlights: Marilla Reservoir, dam, spruce trees

Directions: From downtown Bradford, take PA 346 west for 5.5 miles. A parking area is on the left.

This level and easy trail is ideal for children as it encircles Marilla Reservoir. The reservoir is surrounded by towering spruce trees, creating a wall of green. From the parking area, cross a small bridge over the dam's spillway and proceed across the crest of the dam, where you are treated to nice views of the reservoir. After crossing the dam, turn right and hike above the shore underneath spruce trees. Pass a pavilion and bear right across a long wooden bridge over Marilla Brook as it enters the reservoir. In high water, the reservoir reaches beneath the bridge.

Turn right and proceed along the western shore until the trail crosses a shorter bridge and follows the northern shore. Pass a few picnic tables along the way. The trail returns to the parking area.

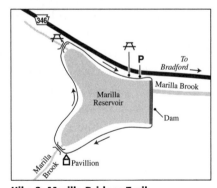

Hike 2: Marilla Bridges Trail

Allegheny National Forest: Bradford Ranger District

The Allegheny National Forest (ANF) is comprised of two ranger districts. The Bradford Ranger District encompasses the northern half of the forest, and the Marienville Ranger District the southern half. The Bradford Ranger District contains most of the hiking trails in the ANF, including Hickory Creek, Tracy Ridge, Minister Creek, Morrison, and most of the North Country Trail, which are some of the most popular.

The Tracy Ridge Hiking Trail System features 33.69 miles of trails. Hikes 6, 7, and 8 can be combined to create a backpacking trip offering mountain streams and beautiful views of the Allegheny Reservoir. Morrison Trail is a 12.3-mile loop with a cross connector trail. Hikes 9 and 10 can be combined for a one-night backpacking trip featuring excellent campsites, beautiful streams, and massive boulders and rock outcrops.

Some of the most scenic trails in this guide are in the Bradford Ranger District, which has massive boulders, cliffs, vistas, waterfalls, old-growth forest, and cascading streams. The trails in this district are also more difficult, particularly near the Allegheny Reservoir and River, where there is greater elevation change.

Contact information: Bradford Ranger District, 29 US Forest Service Drive, Bradford, PA 16701; phone: 814-362-4613. Allegheny National Forest, PO Box 847, Warren, PA 16365; phone: 814-723-5150; websites: www.fs.fed.us/r9/forests/allegheny/ and www.allegheny-online.com/hikingtrails.html.

👥 3. Westline Trail

Duration: 1 to 2 hours

Distance: 2-mile loop

Difficulty: Easy to moderate

Blazes: White/gray diamonds

Terrain: Level and rolling

Elevation change: 80 feet

Trail conditions: Blazes are intermittent and the trail is extremely overgrown, with very little treadway

Highlights: Ledges and rock outcrops

Directions: The road to the trailhead is 2.3 miles east along PA 59 from the juncture of PA 59 and PA 770 at Marshburg and 2.4 miles west along PA 59 from the intersection with US 219. Turn onto FR 455 and drive .2 mile to the main parking area on the left. The trail does not begin there, however; continue .2 mile along the road to FR 320. Turn left and follow FR 320 for .5 mile to the trail sign for the Thundershower Trail on the right. There is limited parking along the road. If FR 320 is gated, park at the main parking area or near the gate, but do not block it. Walk along the road to the trail.

The Westline Trail is for cross-country skiing, so it is not well established or blazed, but it can be hiked. The system covers 9.8 miles, with a variety of loops and linear trails. This route follows sections of Inside-Out, Ledges, and Thundershower Trails.

From FR 320, follow a grassy grade as it descends gradually to the left. Blazes are few, so follow the grade as best you can. Cross a small stream and climb gradually along the grade. Reach a juncture of Inside-Out and Thundershower Trails with a sign. Turn left onto Inside-Out Trail as it gradually descends through open hardwoods. The grade stays above the stream, which is off to your left. It veers right into the woods, where it becomes more defined and follows near the edge of the plateau. Avoid grades that join from the right or descend steeply to the left. The forest opens up and the trail reaches a juncture with Ledges Trail, where there are signs.

Turn left onto Ledges Trail and cross a narrow pipeline swath. The trail passes above massive boulders and ledges that rise above a stream valley. It bends right and passes behind an oil pump, a common sight along much of this trail, which showcases how extensively the ANF is

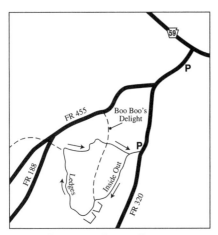

Hike 3: Westline Trail

exploited for its mineral resources. Descend gradually along the overgrown trail and cross the swath. The trail levels and passes another oil pump. Reach a dirt road at a four-way intersection. Continue straight and descend along another dirt road. Pass another pump and reenter the forest to the right; a clear-cut forest is off to the left. This open area contains several roads, pumps, and a storage facility.

Reach the juncture with the Thundershower Trail at a grassy, wide swath. Turn right and hike up the swath. After .2 mile, the trail suddenly leaves the swath to the left and passes through the forest along level terrain. Cross a grassy road and juncture with Boo-Boo's Delight Trail to the left. Continue straight and gradually descend back to the beginning of the loop along another old grade.

4. Timberdoodle Flats Interpretive Trail

Duration: 1½ to 2½ hours

Distance: The system is composed of two loops: the .5-mile Bluebird Loop and the 1.25-mile Woodcock Loop

Difficulty: Easy

Blazes: The Bluebird Loop is blazed with a blue bluebird insignia, and the Woodcock Loop with a yellow woodcock insignia

Terrain: Flat and rolling

Elevation change: 75 feet

Trail conditions: Trails are well established and often grassy; blazes are sparse in places

Highlights: Various forest types, meadows, small streams, hemlocks, wildlife habitats, informative displays

Directions: The parking area is located on the south side of PA 59. It is 5.8 miles west of the intersection of PA 59 and US 219 and 1.2 miles east of the juncture of PA 59 and PA 321 north.

Timberdoodle is a nickname for the American woodcock, one of many birds that live along the trail. The male woodcock is known for its entertaining flight displays during mating season. The trail system is composed of two interlocking loops passing various habitats and forest types. Different animals live in meadows, brush, or mature forests. A variety of nesting boxes and informational displays are erected along the trail. The trail is often wide, grassy, and rolling, making it ideal for children. The Bluebird Loop has a limestone surface.

This property used to be a farm many years ago. The trail provides an excellent example of fields reverting to forest and forest succession. If left undisturbed, the meadows and fields will once again become old-growth forest many years from now.

From the parking area and trail sign with a map and brochures, follow the combined Bluebird and Woodcock Loops to your right. The trail is level as it passes along a meadow to the left. A hardwood forest is to your right. Hike by a pine plantation, and the trail bears right through hardwoods. A short distance farther is a large, gnarled apple tree.

Continue to hike along the wide, grassy trail until you reach an important juncture. To your right, the Bluebird Loop leaves and returns to the parking area after .25 mile. This trail is level and rolling through a young hardwood forest and passes two vernal ponds, seasonal ponds that fill with water in spring and dry in summer; they attract a wide variety of wildlife.

For a longer hike, bear left onto the Woodcock Loop. The trail descends slightly and passes an open meadow with brush piles to your right. Soon after, the trail

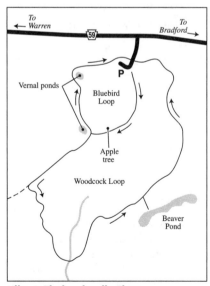

Hike 4: Timberdoodle Flats Interpretive Trail

makes a sudden turn to the left and enters the woods from the wide, grassy, old forest road. Descend slightly through hardwoods until you reach the most scenic part of the trail, a large hemlock and pine forest with small streams and seep springs. The forest is deep and verdant, and you will find it cool even on a hot summer day. The trail curves through this beautiful forest, crossing bridges over small streams.

Begin a mild ascent as the trail leaves the hemlocks. The terrain becomes more level as it passes through open hardwoods. A short side trail to the right leads to a beaver pond. Back on the main loop, enter a large meadow; blazes are infrequent, but the trail crosses the length of the meadow. Expect a lot of sun exposure on a sunny day. Reenter the forest and pass through a pine plantation and an aspen grove. The trail passes through another meadow with an old foundation to the right; PA 59 is also to your right. The trail soon returns you to the parking area.

5. Land of Many Uses Interpretive Trail

Duration: 1 to 2 hours

Distance: 2.6-mile loop

Difficulty: Easy

Blazes: White/gray diamonds

Terrain: Level and rolling

Elevation change: 150 feet

Trail conditions: Trail is generally established, although some blazes may be spaced far apart

Highlights: Rock outcrops and boulders, meadows, springs

Directions: From Smethport, proceed west on PA 59 for 19.4 miles to PA 321. Turn right onto PA 321 north and proceed 10.8 miles to Tracy Ridge Campground. Turn left and follow the road .5 mile to the parking area on the left. From Warren, follow PA 59 east for 20 miles to PA 321 north and turn left; follow the same directions as above. From Bradford, follow PA 346 west for 18 miles. Turn left onto PA 321 south and proceed 3 miles. Turn right into the Tracy Ridge Campground.

This easy loop explores open hardwoods around the Tracy Ridge Campground. From the trailhead, follow the trail across the road to begin the loop. Like the rest of the Tracy Ridge Hiking Trail System, this loop has numbered junctures. Upon reaching No. 1, turn right to begin the loop. Descend through a maze of large moss- and fern-covered boulders. Level terrain follows as the trail explores a hardwood forest. Begin a gradual

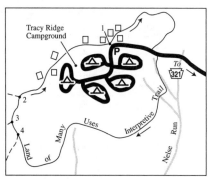

Hike 5: Land of Many Uses Interpretive Trail

ascent to a ridge; a side trail joins from the left. The hardwood forest now has an understory of grass that nearly covers the pathway of the trail. Hike across a large meadow that harbors wildflowers and often deer. Notice the bluebird boxes off to your left. Reenter the forest along the grassy grade and cross the dirt road that accesses the campground.

The trail follows the road to the left for a short distance before turning right and entering the forest. Descend gradually to a scenic spring that flows from the foot of a boulder and creates a small stream. This is the source of Nelse Run, a stream that flows almost 5 miles before emptying into the Allegheny Reservoir. A few hemlock trees grow around the stream. The trail descends along the small stream before turning right and gradually ascending. Pass through smaller boulders and cross another small spring-fed stream. Hike across a few seasonal ravines and climb to the edge of the plateau. The forest remains open, with little vegetation in the understory.

Descend gradually and reach No. 4. Turn right and reach No. 3, and then proceed straight to No. 2. Gradually ascend the plateau along ledges and rock outcrops behind the campground. The trail soon returns to No. 1 and completes the loop.

6. Tracy Ridge and Johnnycake Trails

Duration: 3–5 hours

Distance: 8.7-mile loop

Difficulty: Moderate

Blazes: White/gray diamonds; North Country Trail is blue

Terrain: Flat along the top of the plateau; descents and ascents steepen near the reservoir; sidehill and several small stream crossings

Elevation change: 900 feet

Trail conditions: Trail is well blazed and established; most stream crossings do not have bridges

Highlights: Rock outcrops, Allegheny Reservoir, scenic streams, nice campsites, Johnnycake Run

Directions: From Smethport, proceed west on PA 59 for 19.4 miles to PA 321. Turn right onto PA 321 north and proceed 10.8 miles to Tracy Ridge Campground. Turn left and follow the road .5 mile to the parking area on the left. From Warren, follow PA 59 east for 20 miles to PA 321 north and turn left; follow the same directions as above. From Bradford, follow PA 346 west for 18 miles. Turn left onto PA 321 south and proceed 3 miles. Turn right into the Tracy Ridge Campground.

This 8.7-mile loop was the extent of the Johnnycake–Tracy Ridge Trail system until 1998, when the system was expanded to a 33.69-mile interconnecting system several numbered junctions and renamed the Tracy Ridge Hiking Trail System. This loop continues to be the most popular section of the expanded system.

From the parking area, cross the gravel campground road and turn left at No. 1, passing a side trail to the right that winds through rock outcrops and boulders. The trail is level and begins a slight descent as it passes more rock outcrops and curves behind the campground. Reach juncture No. 2 and bear right. The trail is level as it passes through open hardwoods. Reach No. 15; to the left the trail descends to No. 16, which leads to the Johnnycake Trail at No. 17, or you can turn right onto a new trail following the contour of the plateau to Nos. 13 and 12. The trail is very curvy as it follows the rim of the plateau above the Whiskey Run drainage, and when I hiked here last, it featured no open vistas as indicated on the map. From No. 15, continue on to Nos.

14 and 12 along level terrain. Once you pass No. 12, the trail begins a 400-foot descent to the North Country Trail (NCT) over .7 mile. The trail steepens at the bottom and passes under hemlocks. The NCT joins from the right; if you turn right, there are nice views of the reservoir and beautiful camping where Tracy Run meets the reservoir.

Otherwise, bear left onto the NCT. For the next 2.4 miles, the trail traverses the steep bank of the reservoir, often along a narrow sidehill. The NCT gradually moves farther from the reservoir and crosses seasonal streams, including Whiskey Run. Descend gradually through a pine plantation and reach No. 10, where the Johnnycake Trail joins from the left. Turn left and follow this trail upstream along Johnnycake Run. The ascent is gradual as you proceed up the valley, with hardwoods and two small meadows. Hemlocks become more prevalent, particularly on the slope to the right. Cross the stream without a bridge in a scenic hemlock grove. Hike along an old grade through this scenic grove and cross the run again without a bridge. Climb away from the run into an open hardwood forest.

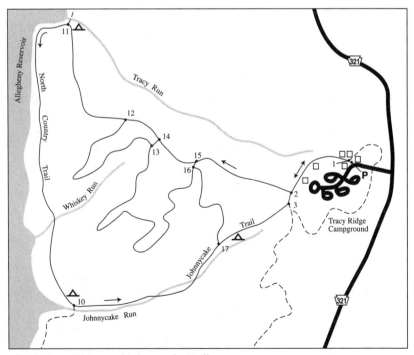

Hike 6: Tracy Ridge and Johnnycake Trails

The trail stays above the run and crosses small, seasonal side streams. Pass No. 17 and continue a gradual climb. Cross another side stream with a nice campsite underneath white pine trees. Hardwoods continue to dominate, but the trail does pass along a few groves of hemlock trees. The climb begins to steepen as you reach the top of the valley. The surrounding hardwood forest is open, with a carpet of grass. The Johnnycake Trail ends at No. 3 and the interpretive trail. Turn left to reach No. 2, the place where you began your hike; return the way you came.

7. Handsome Lake

Duration: 4 to 6 hours

Distance: 9 miles

Difficulty: Moderate to difficult

Blazes: White/gray diamonds

Terrain: Most of the trail is rolling, with gradual descents; a few steep sections

Elevation change: 900 feet

Trail conditions: Trails are generally well blazed and established; the trail is least established, with intermittent blazes, between Nos. 6 and 5

Highlights: Johnnycake Run, hemlocks, Allegheny Reservoir, Handsome Lake Campground

Directions: From Smethport, proceed west on PA 59 for 19.4 miles to PA 321. Turn right onto PA 321 north and proceed 10.8 miles to Tracy Ridge Campground. Turn left and follow the road .5 mile to the parking area on the left. From Warren, follow PA 59 east for 20 miles to PA 321 north and turn left; follow the same directions as above. From Bradford, follow PA 346 west for 18 miles. Turn left onto PA 321 south and proceed 3 miles. Turn right into the Tracy Ridge Campground.

This hike explores the heart of the Tracy Ridge Hiking Trail System. From the parking area, cross the road and proceed to No. 1. Turn left and pass ledges and moss-covered boulders. Gradually descend behind the campground and pass more boulders. At No. 2, turn left to No. 3. At No. 3, turn right to No. 17. The trail descends somewhat steeply through an open hardwood forest with a carpet of grass. As

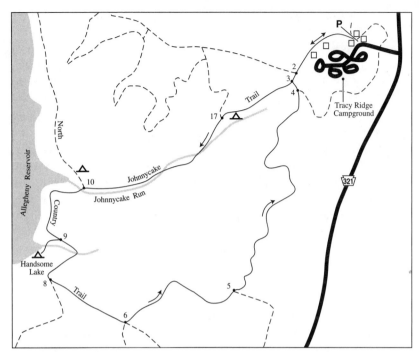

Hike 7: Handsome Lake

you descend more deeply into the valley, the understory becomes thicker and hemlocks become more prevalent in the ravine off to your left. Pass a nice campsite along a small stream and continue to No. 17.

From No. 17, the trail descends more steeply to Johnnycake Run. Cross the run without a bridge in a grove of hemlocks. Hike along an old grade underneath the hemlocks with the run off to your right. This is a scenic part of the trail. Cross the run again without a bridge and pass through two meadows. Return to the run and follow it closely. The Johnnycake Trail ends at its juncture with No. 10 and the North Country Trail (NCT).

Turn left, cross the run, and follow the NCT through a meadow and along narrow sidehill above the reservoir. Hike a steep incline over the ridge, turn left, and the trail is rolling above the reservoir. Bear left onto an old grade and gradually climb along the side of the mountain. The grade turns left, enters a scenic glen with hemlocks, and reaches No. 9. Turn right and descend along a side trail to Handsome Lake Campground. The trail turns left on an old, overgrown paved road and turns right into the campground. Handsome Lake is a fee area featuring beautiful campsites along a peaceful cove. Return the way you came to No. 9.

Continue up the scenic glen underneath hemlocks and pines. The trail turns right, crosses the stream, and steeply ascends the plateau along an old grade. The forest is dominated by hardwoods. At No. 8, follow the NCT as it turns left and traverses the top of a ridge underneath open hardwoods. The ANF's trail map indicates a vista along this section, but there isn't one. After .7 mile, reach No. 6; leave the NCT and turn left on a trail blazed with gray diamonds. This section of trail isn't as well established as the others. Hike across the top of the plateau until the trail bears left and drops to a flat area. Follow the edge of the plateau. The trail is not well established, and the blazes become more infrequent. Turn right where the ANF's trail map indicates another view; again, there isn't one. Gradually ascend underneath some large hemlocks and white pine trees. The trail becomes very unestablished, with infrequent blazes. Continue straight and gradually ascend to the plateau. Drop gradually to No. 5; take the trail to the left. From No. 5 to No. 4 is 2.3 miles. The trail is rolling through open hardwoods. Near the end of this segment, the trail becomes unestablished, with infrequent blazes, and passes through a thick understory of striped maple. Reach No. 4 and continue to the left to No. 3. Retrace your steps to the parking area.

Handsome Lake is not a description of the Allegheny Reservoir; rather, it is the name of a person. Handsome Lake was a Seneca Indian religious prophet, reformer, and half-brother of Chief Cornplanter. At the age of sixty-four, his ministry to the Senecas began with a series of visions. Handsome Lake preached a variety of social and moral beliefs that assisted the Senecas with the transition to life on reservations in a world influenced by Europeans and Americans. His teachings helped maintain Indian values and traditions in a changing world and inspired the creation of the Longhouse Religion, which continues to exist today.

8. Allegheny Reservoir and Nelse Run

Duration: 5 to 7 hours

Distance: 9-mile double loop

Difficulty: Moderate to difficult

Blazes: White/gray diamonds; North Country Trail is blue

Terrain: Several climbs that are steep and long in sections; sidehill along the reservoir

Elevation change: 800 feet

Trail conditions: Variable. North Country Trail is well blazed and established; some trails are somewhat less established or blazed but can still be followed. Trail is blazed with diamond-shaped gray/white placards.

Highlights: Nelse Run, Polly's Run, Allegheny Reservoir, isolation, nice campsites, views of the reservoir

Directions: From Smethport, drive west on PA 59 for 19.4 miles; from Warren, drive east on PA 59 for 20 miles. Turn onto PA 321 north and proceed 7.2 miles to a small parking area on the left. The small lot has parking for four or five cars.

This double loop is the most difficult and scenic trail in the Tracy Ridge Hiking Trail System. As this trail system becomes more popular, you are most likely to find solitude along this route. Highlights are Nelse and Polly's Runs, with beautiful hemlocks and several nice views over the reservoir.

From the parking area along PA 321, descend to Nelse Run and cross the bridge. Nelse Run is a beautiful mountain stream that has carved a gorge graced with hemlocks and pines. It is widely considered to be one of the most scenic areas along the North Country Trail (NCT). Reach the first juncture, No. 7, and turn right, proceeding up Nelse Run's gorge. The trail is level but begins to climb into a side glen, where the trail becomes less established. Cross a small stream underneath hemlocks and pines. Continue to climb, descend into a glen, and cross another small stream. Climb more steeply up the bank underneath pine that gives way to open hardwoods.

The climb continues along trail that is not well established. Reach an old grade and bear left along a more gradual ascent. Reach No. 5 and turn left. For the next 2 miles, the trail is level and rolling along

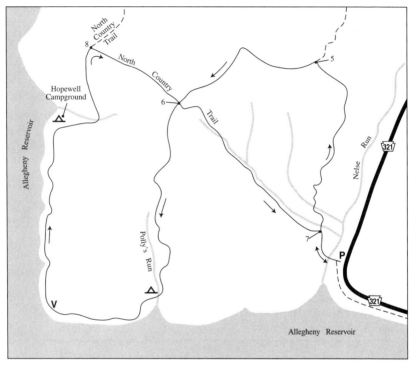

Hike 8: Allegheny Reservoir and Nelse Run

the top of the plateau through open hardwoods. Sections of the trail are not well established or maintained, and blazes are infrequent. There isn't a vista as indicated on ANF's map. Reach a four-way intersection, No. 6, with the NCT, and continue straight on the gray-diamond-blazed trail. Begin a gradual descent and join an old, grassy grade. Descend along this grade; the blazes along here are few. Whenever the grade crosses a wet area, the trail follows sidehill above the grade. Leave the grade and follow sidehill along the contour of the plateau. Enter a small glen and pick up another grade that descends gradually along the side of the plateau. The trail then makes a sharp right turn and descends steeply to Polly's Run. Reach the small stream with boulders, scenic campsites, and hemlocks. Cross the run and climb the bank on the other side.

For the next 3 miles to Hopewell Campground, the trail follows in close proximity to the reservoir. There are many nice views of the reservoir through the trees. The trail is well blazed but relatively unestablished along the bank above the reservoir. This worn-out sidehill can be tough on your ankles, even though the trail is level and rolling. My favorite place is the point at the juncture of Sugar Bay and the reservoir, where there are some beautiful views and a grassy swath of an abandoned pipeline. The trail then bears right and continues above the reservoir with more nice views. Hike around a small bay and continue along the shoreline. As you near Hopewell Campground, the forest becomes more diverse with hemlocks.

Pass behind the campground, which offers picnic tables, campsites, pit toilets, and a water pump. Begin a steep climb up an old grade to the top of a ridge, where the trail meets the NCT at No. 8. Turn right onto the blue-blazed NCT and continue the climb up to the plateau. Reach the top, with level hiking through open hardwoods, and pass the four-way juncture you encountered previously. The terrain remains level but begins a gradual descent that steepens along an old grade into a side glen of Nelse Run's gorge. The forest transforms into deep hemlock and pine, with small streams and springs descending from the slope to your right. Continue to descend gradually along this grade into this beautiful gorge. The trail soon reaches the bottom; cross the bridge and return to your car.

9. Morrison Trail Loop (Morrison Trail)

Duration: 2 to 4 hours

Distance: 5.3-mile loop

Difficulty: Moderate

Blazes: White/gray diamonds

Terrain: Ascents and descents tend to be gradual along streams with a few steep sections; often rocky

Elevation change: 600 feet

Trail conditions: Well established trail is blazed with gray, diamond-shaped placards and old, faded blue blazes. Trail is well established. Several stream crossings without bridges.

Highlights: Massive boulders and outcrops, small waterfalls and cascades, Morrison Run, beautiful streams, excellent backcountry campsites

Directions: The trailhead has plentiful parking. It is located along PA 59, almost 27 miles west of Smethport and 13.5 miles east of Warren.

The Morrison Trail is an 11-mile loop divided by a 1.3-mile cross connector trail. This essentially divides the trail in two loops, a 5.3-mile east loop known as the Morrison Trail Loop, and an 8.3-mile western loop known as the Rimrock Trail Loop, as identified on the ANF's Morrison Trail map. These two loops are described as separate day hikes; the entire trail system can be hiked as a backpacking trail and is one of the national forest's most scenic and popular trails.

From the parking area, follow a connector trail along a seasonal stream. Cross the stream and continue a gradual descent through open hardwood forests to the beginning of the loop near some outcrops. Follow the trail to the right and descend more steeply to the small stream. Cross the stream and follow the crossconnector trail to the left. This 1.3-mile trail crosses the stream three times and offers incredible scenery. Descend closely along the small stream. Cross the stream and pick up an old grade. Here the boulders become more prevalent. The trail makes a sudden right turn away from the obvious grade and descends through the massive boulders. Pass near one scenic cascade

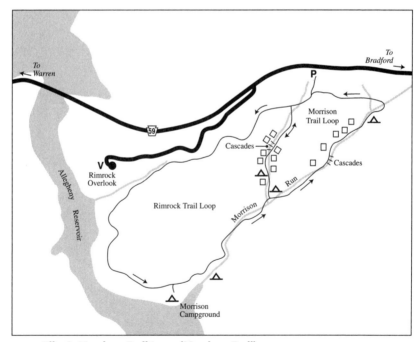

Hike 9: Morrison Trail Loop (Morrison Trail)
Hike 10: Rimrock Trail Loop (Morrison Trail)

formed by massive, jumbled boulders clogging the stream. Cross the stream and continue to gradually descend, passing massive, house-size boulders covered with moss, ferns, and even trees growing from the top. Along this section of trail are hemlocks and meadows offering beautiful campsites.

Continue the gradual descent and cross the stream underneath thick hemlocks; the grade mentioned previously joins from the left. Pass more campsites; reach the main loop and Morrison Run.

Cross Morrison Run and rejoin the loop. Turn left and proceed upstream along beautiful Morrison Run; the trail crosses the run four times. This beautiful stream tunnels through thick hemlocks with small cascades and pools. At times the trail follows the remnants of an old grade. As you hike upstream, large boulders and outcrops become more prevalent, though they never reach the size of those along the crossconnector trail. Several campsites lie along the stream, as well as cascades and small waterfalls. Pass a meadow, cross the stream, and begin a 150-foot climb out of the valley. Cross a small side stream and hike across rolling terrain underneath open hardwoods with a thick understory of mountain laurel. Descend gradually, pass a few outcrops, and reach the connector trail. Turn right and return to your car.

10. Rimrock Trail Loop (Morrison Trail)

Duration: 4 to 7 hours

Distance: 8.3-mile loop

Difficulty: Moderate to difficult

Blazes: White/gray diamonds

Terrain: Variable between level hiking on top of the plateau and steep terrain along Campbell Run; extensive streamside and sidehill hiking

Elevation change: 700 feet

Trail conditions: Trail is well blazed and established; there are several stream crossings without bridges

Highlights: Allegheny Reservoir, Morrison Run, massive boulders and outcrops, scenic streams, beautiful campsites

Directions: The trailhead has plentiful parking. It is located along PA 59, almost 27 miles west of Smethport and 13.5 miles east of Warren.

The Morrison Trail is an 11-mile loop divided by a 1.3-mile cross connector trail. This essentially divides the trail in two loops, a 5.3-mile east loop known as the Morrison Trail Loop, and an 8.3-mile western loop known as the Rimrock Trail Loop, as identified on the ANF's Morrison Trail map. These two loops are described as separate day hikes. The entire trail system offers excellent backpacking and is one of the national forest's most scenic and popular trails.

From the parking area, follow a connector trail along a seasonal stream. Cross the stream and continue a gradual descent through open hardwood forests to the beginning of the loop near some outcrops. Follow the trail to the right and descend more steeply to the small stream. Cross the stream and pass the crossconnector trail to the left, which will be the return route to this spot. Climb gradually away from the stream, and cross the level and rolling terrain along the top of the plateau for almost 2 miles. The forest here is dominated by oak, hickory, and other hardwoods, with an understory of laurel and brush. Sections of this trail are brushy.

Reach the headwaters of Campbell Run and begin to descend along the left side of the run. This is a 400-foot descent over .8 mile. Campbell Run is a small stream with cascades; it is reduced to a trickle in summer. The trail bears left away from the run and follows the contour of the plateau above the reservoir for about 1.5 miles. Pass a side trail to the right that leads down to Morrison Campground, with campsites, pit toilets, water pump, and a small beach. It is one of the most scenic camping areas along the reservoir and can be reached only by foot or boat. A small fee is required to stay at the campground.

Back on the trail, cross a small stream and hike along the side of the mountain down to Morrison Run. At the run, notice an established side trail marked with faded blue blazes heading downstream. This trail has beautiful campsites and reaches the reservoir. For the next 1.5 miles, proceed upstream along scenic Morrison Run, with small cascades, pools, boulders, and hemlocks. Reach the juncture with the crossconnector trail, and turn left onto it. For the next 1.3 miles, proceed upstream along this stream, with three stream crossings. Pass campsites and hike underneath hemlocks. Cross the stream; a grade continues straight ahead. Continue a gradual ascent, passing massive, house-size boulders with open meadows and more campsites. Cross the stream again below cascades formed by huge boulders clogging the run. Climb among the boulders to the old grade, where the trail turns left. Follow the grade above the stream until the trail crosses the stream again. Follow the stream closely until you reach the juncture with the other side of the loop, then turn right and return to your car.

 # 11. Rimrock Overlook

Duration: ½ hour

Distance: .2 mile

Difficulty: Easy to moderate

Blazes: None

Terrain: Level and rolling, with steep descents and ascents through cliffs and boulders

Elevation change: 100 feet

Trail conditions: Trails are well established but not blazed. There are many established, intersecting trails around Rimrock, which can be confusing.

Highlights: Spectacular vistas, cliffs, massive boulders, crevasses, cold-air vents, rock outcrops and formations

Directions: From Warren, take PA 59 east for 12.7 miles. Along the way, you will cross the bridge over the Allegheny Reservoir. Turn right onto FR 454 and drive 2.7 miles to the end of the road, where there is a parking and picnic area.

Of the three developed overlooks in the ANF, Rimrock provides the finest view and is a popular destination within the forest. It also offers much more than views. A short trail system takes you down a rock staircase through a narrow crevasse and past spectacular cliffs, boulders, and in the summer, deep fractures that emit cold air.

From the parking area, follow an obvious trail along boardwalks and steps down along ledges and boulders. In front of one smooth boulder is a concrete bench; remember this juncture, because you will return to this spot along a trail that joins from the left. Reach another boardwalk and steps that lead down to the overlook. From here you can see a wide expanse of the reservoir and surrounding plateaus. The setting is almost completely undisturbed. Rimrock is about 700 vertical feet above the reservoir.

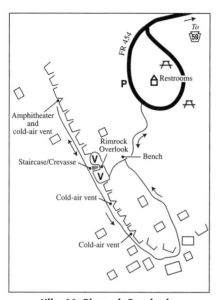

Hike 11: Rimrock Overlook

From the overlook, follow a narrow stone staircase that descends through a crevasse capped with a boulder. In some places, the crevasse is a little more than two feet wide. This staircase takes you to the bottom of the cliffs; turn right and follow along the base of the cliffs. After a few hundred feet, reach a rock amphitheater with a deep, dark crevasse. In summer, a strong cold-air vent is located here. Such vents are created by the rocks being cooled over the winter. In summer, the air descends through the crevasses, is cooled, and flows out the bottom. This particular vent is strong enough to create condensation on glasses. A trail continues along the base of the cliffs but becomes less established as it climbs up the hill back to the parking area.

Turn around and return to the staircase. If you hear water flowing, it is from spring that flows about 100 feet below the trail. From the end of the staircase, continue straight along the bottom of the cliffs and pass two more cold-air vents. Look down below the trail to see massive boulders and outcrops, some shaped like triangles or pyramids. The trail begins to bear left underneath a fascinating rock column before scrambling up along boulders and outcrops. There is an established trail, but many others intersect. Follow the trail that climbs around the cliffs, keeping the boulders about 20 feet off to your left. These off-trail boulders, with crevasses and overhangs, offer some great exploration. Reach the top and bear left with boulders off to your left. The trail rejoins the other at the bench.

It is believed that Chief Cornplanter once owned Rimrock, and some speculate his famous, if not mythical, cave may be located at the overlook. Rimrock contains small caves between the outcrops and boulders off the trail.

🚶‍♂️🚶 12. Jakes Rocks

Duration: 1 hour

Distance: 1-mile trail system

Difficulty: Easy to moderate

Blazes: None

Terrain: Level to rolling

Elevation change: 120 feet

Trail conditions: Trails on top of the plateau from the parking area to the views are paved and level. Trails that descend to the bottom of the cliffs are established but steep and narrow in sections.

Highlights: Views, cliffs, massive boulders and outcrops, crevasses, rock overhangs, Indian Cave

Directions: From Kinzua Point Information Center along PA 59, follow the Longhouse Scenic Byway (FR 262) for 1.2 miles. Turn right onto FR 492 and follow for 1.1 miles and turn right. Follow the road to Jakes Rocks for .8 mile, then turn right and proceed .2 mile to the last parking area along the road.

I had been to Jakes Rocks twice before arriving a third time to research the trail for this book. During my previous visits, I did not realize an established trail led to the bottom of the cliffs to reveal some of the most impressive cliffs, boulders, crevasses, and rock overhangs in the ANF. The true highlight of Jakes Rocks is not its views, but what lies beneath them.

From the end of the last parking area, follow a paved trail across level and rolling terrain. Pass a few boulders underneath a hardwood forest with a thick understory of mountain laurel and brush. Shortly before reaching the vista, pass a side trail to the left that descends to a cluster of boulders; this trail then bears left and goes underneath a small overhang, beneath the vista. This vista is from a rock outcrop, providing a narrow view of the reservoir to the north.

From the vista, follow the paved trail as it loops around the side of the plateau. Just after leaving the vista, look to your right to see a narrow, unblazed trail ascending through mountain laurel; keep this trail and juncture in mind.

The trail passes more boulders, with short side trails to the right that lead to narrow vistas. You are right above cliffs to the right, so do

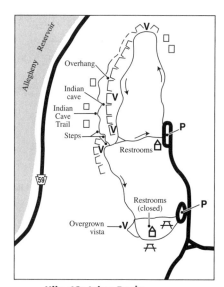

Hike 12: Jakes Rocks

not venture too far off the trail. Pass larger boulders before reaching two paved trails to the left; these trails go back to the parking area. The trail then passes another vista to the right, which offers an overgrown view to the west of the reservoir and dam. Notice an established side trail to the right that descends from the vista along stone steps to the bottom of the cliffs. Although there isn't a sign, this trail is known as the Indian Cave Trail; follow this trail down to the base of the cliffs. Pass impressive cliffs, boulders, crevasses, and rock overhangs. Reach one massive overhang that shelters a massive boulder; a narrow crevasse lies behind the boulder. The scenery is outstanding. The trail narrows and descends. Pass another overhang with another crevasse and boulder. It is possible to hike through this crevasse.

From here, the trail is narrow and more eroded. It is best to retrace your steps along the Indian Cave Trail; otherwise, hike along the cliffs, with more boulders and outcrops. The trail continues to narrow and ascends along the side of the mountain. It becomes little more than a deer path as it climbs through brush and laurel before rejoining the paved trail near the first vista, at the juncture mentioned previously.

Back at the second vista, the paved trail continues on to another vista, which is completely overgrown. Soon thereafter, the trail passes a picnic area and locked restrooms. The trail ends at another parking area. To return to your car, retrace your steps along the paved trail to the second vista or hike across the parking area and turn left onto the road. There are three more vistas along the road leaving Jakes Rocks.

13. Bent Run Waterfalls

Duration: 1/2 hour

Distance: .2 mile (one-way)

Difficulty: Moderate

Blazes: None

Terrain: Rocky glen with large boulders and some steep areas

Elevation change: 150 feet

Trail conditions: Trail is unblazed and becomes less established as it heads upstream along the run

Highlights: Small waterfalls, cascades, large boulders and outcrops, views of the Allegheny Reservoir and Kinzua Dam

Directions: From the Kinzua Dam, proceed .3 mile east on PA 59 to a parking area and trail sign on the right

Bent Run is a small stream, a little over a mile long. It descends 700 feet from the top of the plateau to the Allegheny Reservoir through a rugged glen with boulders, outcrops, waterfalls, and cascades. In dry weather, this small stream is reduced to a trickle. Most waterfalls are formed by resistant rock layers the stream encounters as it descends. The Bent Run waterfalls, however, exist because the streambed has a steep gradient that is clogged with large boulders. This is common in the ANF.

From the gravel parking area, hike up the established path along the stream, which flows to your right. There aren't any blazes along this trail. Notice the numerous cascades that tumble down the boulder-clogged streambed. The highest cascades are near the parking area. Some of the boulders are massive and have trees growing on top, supported by webs of roots

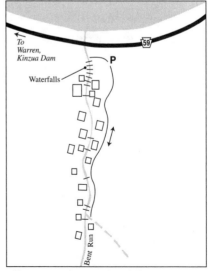

Hike 13: Bent Run Waterfalls

and coatings of moss or ferns. As you hike upstream, pass a hidden 6-foot falls tumbling from a boulder. Continue to climb along the trail along a staircase of cascades.

You will reach a sloping 3- to 4-foot cascade across a tilted boulder into a pool. From here, the trail becomes less established as it traverses the steep, eroded bank along the run. It may be best to simply rock-hop along the boulders that clog the stream. Climb further to a jumbled maze of boulders through which the run has carved little chasms. The trail ends where a seasonal side stream joins from the left with a 5-foot falls. Return the way you came. Back at the parking area, enjoy the nice views of the reservoir and dam.

14. Little Boulder Nature Trail

Duration: 1/2 hour	
Distance: .25-mile semiloop trail	
Difficulty: Easy	
Blazes: None	
Terrain: Rolling	
Elevation change: 50 feet	
Trail conditions: Trail is not blazed but is well established	
Highlights: Boulders, hemlocks, numbered stations, scenic woodlands	
Directions: From the US 6 and PA 59 juncture near Warren, proceed east on PA 59. Go 5.7 miles to the Big Bend Visitors Center on the left. There is a trail sign across from the visitor center parking lot.	

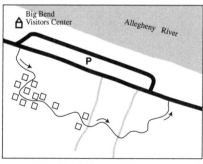

Hike 14: Little Boulder Nature Trail

This trail is excellent for children, who will be fascinated by the boulders and webs of roots from trees that grow on top of them. It features a total of twelve numbered stations that correspond to a guide. The trail enters a scenic hemlock forest and winds through clusters of car-size boulders that harbor ferns, moss, and trees. The surrounding forest is lush and verdant. Near station No. 7 is a boulder with a small overhang that children would enjoy crawling beneath.

The trail continues along the hillside, crossing bridges over seasonal streams and springs. This section of trail does not have as many boulders, and the forest is dominated by hardwoods with fewer hemlocks. Descend to the road and parking area. Turn left and walk back to your car.

15. Smorgasbord Forest Trail

Duration: 1 hour

Distance: .33 mile (one-way)

Difficulty: Easy to moderate

Blazes: None

Terrain: Level and rolling, with one moderate ascent and descent

Elevation change: 100 feet

Trail conditions: Trail is wide, with mowed grass

Highlights: Kinzua Dam, interpretive trail with numbered stations, views of the dam and gorge, waterfall

Directions: From the US 6 and PA 59 juncture near Warren, proceed east on PA 59. Go 5.7 miles to the Big Bend Visitors Center. Park in the first parking area upon turning off PA 59. A sign marks the beginning of the trail.

This is an interesting trail, featuring the Kinzua Dam and numbered stations that relate to a guide describing the various trees along the trail. The trail follows a wide, grassy path along a grade. Upon reaching station No. 6, the trail begins a moderate climb that levels off right along PA 59. Hike along the road. At station No. 15, a power line and tower to your left are a favorite resting spot for turkey vultures. Continue a short distance to station No. 18; look across the road to view a spring-fed waterfall cascading 50 feet down a cliff carved along PA 59. This falls flows year-round and may be the highest in the ANF. Other seasonal springs descend from this cliff as well. In winter, this area is popular with ice climbers.

Reach the viewing platforms overlooking the dam and river. The Kinzua Dam was completed in 1965 and forms the Allegheny Reser-

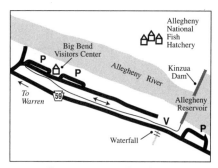

Hike 15: Smorgasbord Forest Trail

voir. No other structure has had such a profound impact on the ANF as this dam and the reservoir created by it. The Kinzua Dam is 179 feet high and 1,877 feet long. In summer, the Allegheny Reservoir is 24.2 miles long and covers 12,080 acres. On top of the mountain above the dam is the massive, circular Seneca Power Reservoir. Water is pumped up to this reservoir and then drained to generate electricity during peak hours; the peak generating capacity is 400,000 kilowatts per hour. Fishing and canoeing are very popular below the dam. An ideal canoe trip is from the Big Bend Visitors Center down to Warren, where the river flows through a canyon with numerous islands and boulders. Bald eagles are commonly seen around the dam.

Behind the dam, schools of carp often assemble. They enjoy eating bread that people throw to them from the top of the dam. Across the river is the Allegheny National Fish Hatchery, where 620,000 fingerling lake trout and 100,000 brook trout are raised every year. The hatchery is also home to 3,000 brood stock lake trout. There forty raceways outside, forty-eight tanks inside, and the facility uses about 8 million gallons of water a day. The hatchery is a great place to take children to learn about fish and is open 9 A.M. to 3 P.M. daily.

16. Campbell Mill Loop Interpretive Trail

Duration: 2 hours

Distance: 1.5-mile loop

Difficulty: Moderate

Blazes: White/gray diamonds

Terrain: Level and rolling, with a few ascents and descents that are steep in sections

Elevation change: 300 feet

Trail conditions: Trail is generally well blazed but not well established in many sections. There is usually a treadway to follow; however, there are blowdowns along the trail, overgrown sections, and some stinging nettle in moist areas.

Highlights: Dewdrop Run, massive boulders, cascades

Directions: From the juncture of PA 59 and US 6 near Warren, proceed 9 miles east on PA 59. Turn right onto Longhouse National Scenic Byway. After 2.9 miles, pass the entrance of Dewdrop Recreation Area and park alongside the road where it bends over Dewdrop Run. Parking is very limited. You can park at the recreation area, but a fee is required.

This trail is a loop that passes through the Dewdrop Recreation Area. There is a fee to park in the recreation area, so this hike begins along the Longhouse Scenic Byway. From the road, notice a gray diamond-shaped placard on a tree. Descend from the road and pass through a meadow where the trail is overgrown. Enter the forest, with open hardwoods, and cross over a side stream. The terrain is rolling as the trail explores the side of the glen above Dewdrop Run, which flows off to your left. After about .3 mile, the trail turns left and descends to Dewdrop Run.

This is the scenic highlight of the trail. Reach the stream above a cluster of boulders, where there are cascades. Follow Dewdrop Run closely and hike upstream; the run flows alongside and underneath massive house-size boulders. In places, the boulders overhang the run. The trail is very close to the run and can be flooded in high water. Climb away from the run as the trail winds through huge boulders. At this point, the trail leaves Dewdrop Run, but you can bushwhack upstream to see other cascades; there is a faint trail on the right side of the run heading upstream. If you decide to bushwhack upstream, you will find a 7-foot cascade and small pool .1 mile upstream and a 4-foot cascade about .2 mile upstream.

Back on the trail, the route winds through more massive boulders, and the trail becomes less estab-

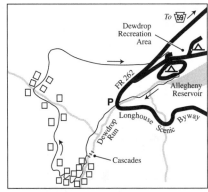

Hike 16: Campbell Mill Loop Interpretive Trail

lished. Climb around and between the boulders up the side of the mountain. The trail levels off as it maintains its elevation along the side of the glen. There are large boulders off to your left. The trail bends left and climbs more steeply along an old grade into the glen of a side stream. Near the top of this glen, the trail bends right and crosses a spring that flows from the large rocks and boulders. Continue a more moderate ascent into the open forest, where the trail is not well established but is well blazed. Reach the edge of the plateau and descend to an old grade, where the trail turns right. Follow this old grade as it gradually descends. Near the Longhouse Scenic Byway, another grade joins from the right. Descend steeply along the bank above the byway and cross the road to the left.

Continue the descent until the trail reaches another grade and turns left. Follow this grade to a water treatment facility. Here the blazes disappear. At the facility, turn right and follow the access road down to the paved road, where the trail turns left and goes along the road downhill. Before reaching the information booth, turn right onto the paved campground road and then turn right again. Hike the road down through the campground. At campsite No. 12, the trail turns right and leaves the road. Pass through this campsite and hike behind campsite No. 10 along a sandy inlet of the Allegheny Reservoir.

Reach Dewdrop Run and cross it without a bridge. Proceed closely upstream along this scenic stream, keeping an eye out for brook trout. Cross a side stream and then cross the run again without a bridge. Climb the bank, cross the road, and return to your car.

🚶🚶 17. Longhouse Interpretive Trail

Duration: 1½ to 2½ hours	
Distance: 2-mile loop	
Difficulty: Moderate	
Blazes: White/gray diamonds	
Terrain: Descents and ascents tend to be moderate, with short steep sections	
Elevation change: 300 feet	
Trail conditions: Trail is in very poor condition, most of it is overgrown with many blowdowns. One section is poorly blazed, and some sections have infrequent blazes.	

Highlights: Hiking along the Allegheny Reservoir

Directions: From the juncture of PA 59 and FR 262 (Longhouse Scenic Byway) near Kinzua Point, follow FR 262 for 10.1 miles to a small pull-off on the left where the trail begins. This is just beyond the entrance to the Kiasutha Recreation Area. From the juncture of FR 262 and PA 321 near Red Bridge, follow FR 262 for 1.3 miles.

The Longhouse Interpretive Trail is a 2-mile loop that begins and ends at the Kiasutha Recreation Area. Beginning at the recreation area will require paying a fee, so this hike begins along the Longhouse Scenic Byway.

From your car, cross the road and scramble up the bank. The trail bends right and gradually ascends. It is well blazed but not well established. Cross a narrow power line swath, where the trail becomes very brushy. Begin a winding ascent up the side of the plateau. Blazes tend to be infrequent, but they can be followed. After several turns during this ascent, the trail bends left and maintains its elevation along old, overgrown grades. Hardwoods dominate the forest, with a relatively thick understory of brush. Cross a seasonal stream and continue to follow the old grades. The trail enters a fern meadow, where there are no blazes, or treadway. From the last blaze, bear slightly left downhill. Continue to bear slightly downhill along the contour of the plateau when you reenter the forest. Look down ahead to see more blazes.

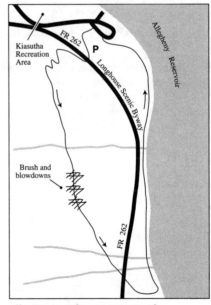

Begin a long, gradual descent from the plateau. The trail crosses several springs and seasonal streams. Cross the narrow powerline swath, and the trail bears left and descends the bank to the Longhouse Scenic Byway. Cross the road and reenter the forest. This is the most scenic section of the trail, as it follows the bank above the reservoir with several views. At times

Hike 17: Longhouse Interpretive Trail

the trail is very narrow and close to the steep banks of the reservoir. Cross several small seasonal streams with bridges. The forest is also scenic, with a mixture of hemlocks and hardwoods. The trail moves away from the reservoir and reaches a parking area. Turn left and hike along the parking area. The trail soon leaves the parking area to the left and gradually ascends until it reaches a clear-cut area. Turn left along the clear-cut and gradually ascend back to your car and the Longhouse Scenic Byway.

18. Hector Falls

Duration: 1 to 2 hours	
Distance: .9 mile (one-way)	
Difficulty: Easy to moderate	
Blazes: None	
Terrain: Gradual descents and ascents	
Elevation change: 200 feet	
Trail conditions: Trail follows gated forestry road and clearly established trail along Hector Run	
Highlights: Hector Falls, massive boulders, and outcrops with crevasses and caves	
Directions: From Warren, drive 17 miles east on US 6 to Ludlow. Turn right onto South Hillside Avenue (also called South Hillside Road). Turn left onto Water Street and then right onto Scenic Drive. Cross the railroad tracks where the road changes from asphalt, and follow FR 133 for 1 mile. Turn right onto FR 258 and follow it for 2.1 miles, until you reach gated FR 258H on the left. There is some space to park, but do not block the gate.	

Despite its isolation, Hector Falls is a popular place to hike. The trail follows a gated forest road as it descends through a mixed forest of hardwoods and hemlocks. The forest off to your right is more open. After about .5 mile, the road passes a deer fence surrounding a forest with a thick understory of saplings. The road curves to the right and passes an open area to the right that appears to be an old gravel pit. Then the road curves to the left and continues its descent.

Upon reaching a Y, turn left and descend more steeply. The road ends at a gas well in a grassy glade. Notice small boulders and the beginning of the trail to the right. The trail is clearly established but not blazed. It passes under thick hemlocks next to a small, sandy stream to your left.

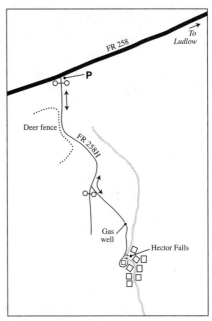

The trail leads to Hector Falls, a 22-foot waterfall that descends over a cliff. Huge boulders and outcrops surround the falls, some with crevasses and caves. Although not very high, Hector Falls is unique in that there are few, if any, other falls tumbling over the sandstone and conglomerate cliffs and boulders that are so common in the ANF. Most of the streams are not large enough to create falls, and those that are flow through the many cracks, fissures, and crevasses that are common with these outcrops, rather than over the edge of them.

Hike 18: Hector Falls

In fact, this is slowly happening to Hector Falls. In low water, the stream descends through a narrow fissure on the left. This run usually has some water year-round.

Downstream from the falls are massive boulders. The streambed is very sandy and the small stream takes an almost subterranean route as it flows underneath and through narrow crevasses of the huge boulders. After enjoying the beauty of the falls and its surroundings, return the way you came.

19. Deer Lick Trail

Duration: 2 to 3 hours

Distance: 5.5-mile double loop

Difficulty: Moderate

Blazes: Blue

Terrain: Flat and rolling, with gradual ascents and descents

Elevation change: 350 feet

Trail conditions: There is generally a treadway, but some sections are brushy; blazes are spaced far apart in sections

Highlights: Scenic streams, scenic woodlands, isolation, hemlocks

Directions: From the juncture of US 6 and PA 948 at Sheffield, proceed east on US 6 for .7 mile. Turn left onto Toll Gate Road and drive .1 mile to a small parking area on the right.

Deer Lick is another of the ANF's cross-country skiing trails. As a result, expect to find blazes far apart and brushy sections along the trail. Most stream crossings have bridges. Deer Lick offers great woodland scenery, scenic streams, and surprising isolation despite being so close to US 6 and Sheffield.

From the parking area, hike up the road and pass a private campground to the right. After .3 mile, reach a cabin and gated road to the left. This gated road will be your return route. Cross a bridge over Deer Lick Run and pass another cabin to the right. Continue straight onto a gated, grassy forest road. After a few hundred yards, the trail splits at a sign; this is the Reservoir Loop. Turn right and follow an old jeep road up a short incline. The trail turns left and follows an old grade. For the next mile, follow the level grade underneath hemlocks, and cross small streams and seep springs with many old pipelines.

Reach a juncture with the Pipeline Loop. Turn left and continue on the Reservoir Loop as it descends through scenic hemlocks. Turn right to begin the Deer Lick Loop, a 3-mile loop. Hike an old grade along Deer Lick Run. Reach the beginning of the loop where the trail splits; turn right. For the next 1.2 miles, the trail gradually ascends along an old grade. The trail is least established along this section. The forest is primarily hardwoods, and the trail crosses the stream once. Reach a gravel forest road and turn left.

The road makes a short, easy ascent before beginning a long, gradual descent. It becomes grassy and passes through a deep hemlock forest along the side of the valley.

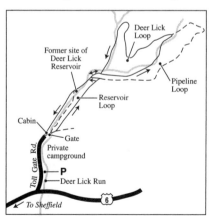

Hike 19: Deer Lick Trail

The trail turns left; keep an eye out for the blazes and a trail sign, as this turn is easy to miss. You now begin to hike along the most scenic section of the trail. The trail gradually descends along an old grade, passing a cascading spring to the left. Hike down the valley, crossing Deer Lick Run as it meanders from one side to the other. The forest is dominated by deep hemlocks and is very scenic. Cross the run twice across bridges. Reach the beginning of the loop and retrace your steps to the Reservoir Loop.

At the Reservoir Loop, proceed straight and cross the run and small side streams. Pass a large meadow to the left; according to the map, this is the former site of the Deer Lick Reservoir, which has been drained. At the end of this meadow, the trail turns left and crosses the run, but this turn is difficult to locate. Instead, proceed straight and hike along the unblazed road as it passes through large meadows. The road stays above the run, which is off to your left. Leave the meadows and enter the forest. The road gradually descends to the gate and cabin. Follow the road back to the parking area.

20. Tionesta National Scenic Area

Duration: 1 hour

Distance: 1-mile loop

Difficulty: Easy

Blazes: White/gray diamonds; North Country Trail is blazed blue

Terrain: Rolling

Elevation change: 100 feet

Trail conditions: Trail is very brushy, with several blowdowns and debris; several small stream crossings

Highlights: Spectacular old-growth hemlock forest

Directions: From Warren, drive 17 miles east on US 6 to Ludlow. Turn right onto South Hillside Avenue (also called South Hillside Road). Turn left onto Water Street and then right onto Scenic Drive. Cross the railroad tracks where the road changes from asphalt, and follow FR 133 for 4.1 miles to a bridge over Tionesta Creek. It is difficult to follow this road, because other dirt roads join it and it is not always clear which one to take, as they are not marked with signs. If any road joins with a stop sign, do not take it. After crossing the bridge, follow FR 133 for 1.6 miles; turn right onto 133E and follow for 1 mile to the scenic area.

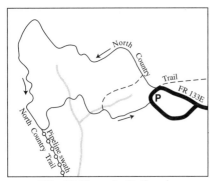

Hike 20: Tionesta National Scenic Area

The Tionesta National Scenic Area encompasses one of the largest old-growth forests in the eastern United States. It was also recognized as a national natural landmark in 1977. Despite these qualities, the scenic area appears to be forgotten, probably because of its isolation. The trails can be followed but are not well established. There are several blowdowns, and branches litter the trails. The scenic area also suffered a direct hit from the infamous 1985 tornado, which destroyed many trees and left open swaths in the forest that are now filled with tree saplings. The trails are very curvy and make a few small stream crossings.

From the parking area, follow the North Country Trail along level terrain. After a few hundred yards, a cross connector trail joins from the left. Continue on the North Country Trail as it tunnels through thick birch saplings. After several twists and turns, you reach a beautiful expanse of massive hemlocks, that rise like columns into the canopy. Notice how open the forest is in sections, thanks to the tornado. The trail explores part of the old growth before diving back into the saplings. Continue to follow the trail as it twists through the saplings and magnificent old-growth trees.

The North Country Trail then reaches a grassy pipeline swath and turns left. It follows the swath, which is interspersed with huge hemlocks, for a short distance before turning left and reentering the forest. The trail continues south along the swath tunneling through the saplings. Descend and pass the cross connector trail. Cross a small stream and climb up to the parking area.

🚶🚶 21. Minister Creek

Duration 4 to 6 hours

Distance: 7.3-mile loop

Difficulty: Moderate

Blazes: White/gray diamonds

Terrain: The trail is located in Minister Creek's steep-sided valley. The terrain is mostly rolling, with a few steep sections, and is rocky in several places.

Elevation change: 400 feet

Trail conditions: Trail is blazed with gray diamond-shaped placards. It is well established and often follows sidehill and old grades. Most stream crossings have bridges.

Highlights: Minister Creek, excellent campsites, massive rock outcrops and boulders, crevasses, Minister Valley Overlook, North Country Trail, Tionesta Creek

Directions: From Sheffield, drive almost 15 miles west along PA 666 to a large parking area on the left. From East Hickory, drive 19 miles east along PA 666; the parking area will be on your right.

Minister Creek is one of the most scenic and popular trails in the national forest. It is not only an excellent day hike, but also a great short, one-night backpacking trail. The trail has two backcountry campsites, and the north end of the loop connects with the North Country Trail. Minister Creek Campground is located across from the parking area and has six sites, water pumps, picnic tables, and pit toilets.

From the parking area, bear left onto PA 666 and turn right onto the trail. Follow an old, wide grade as it gradually ascends underneath hemlocks to the beginning of the loop, which is marked by a trail sign. Turn right and make a rocky descent to Minister Creek. An unblazed trail joining from the right goes down to the campground along the creek.

The trail follows the creek upstream and crosses it over a bridge. Minister Creek has excellent water quality and offers fine backcountry trout fishing. Begin a steep, short ascent up the side of the valley. The trail bears left and follows sidehill along the side of the valley, above the creek. Notice the open meadows along the creek. Begin to gradually bear right along the contour of the valley as the trail enters the glen of a side stream. Boulders and outcrops appear along the trail. To

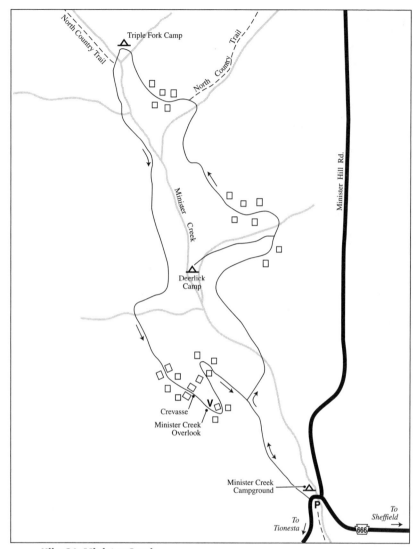

Hike 21: Minister Creek

the left, pass a side trail that descends to Deerlick Camp, one of two backcountry sites along the trail. Cross a small stream with more massive boulders and outcrops. The trail continues to follow along the contour of the valley.

Cross another stream and pass more impressive boulders. The North Country Trail joins from the right. Descend to Minister Creek and reach Triple Fork Camp, another backcountry area offering beautiful camping. Cross a stream, pass through a meadow, and cross over Minister Creek. The North Country Trail leaves to the right. Your trail bears left and follows an old grade along the creek. Enter a grove of hemlocks and cross another creek. Continue to follow Minister Creek downstream with beautiful scenery. The trail turns right and makes a rocky ascent, until it bears left and follows the contour of the valley. Enter a glen, cross a side stream, and begin another climb among boulders and outcrops.

As you continue to gain elevation, massive boulders, cliffs, and outcrops rise along the trail, which at one point passes through an impressive crevasse between a cliff and monstrous boulder. Reach the edge of the plateau and follow the trail to beautiful Minister Creek Overlook, where you can view the valley and plateau from an exposed cliff. From the overlook, the trail descends steeply, winding through crevasses, outcrops, and rock overhangs. Continue to descend more gradually along switchbacks. Turn right onto an old grade, which returns you to the beginning of the loop. From here, follow the trail down to your car.

From the parking area, you can make a very enjoyable short side trip down to beautiful Tionesta Creek, where you can wade, fish, or simply soak up the scenery. Pass the gate and follow a grade downstream along Minister Creek through a grove of hemlocks and pines. Eventually the grade diminishes, but keep heading downstream, with Minister Creek off to your left, until you reach the large, scenic Tionesta Creek. The terrain is level, but sandy and often wet. This side trail offers several excellent potential campsites. Tionesta Creek is an excellent canoe trip and offers more isolation than the more popular Clarion and Allegheny Rivers.

Because of its sublime scenery, Minister Creek is heavily visited and often crowded. Please treat this special place with respect so that others may enjoy it too.

22. Hearts Content National Scenic Area

Duration: 1 to 2 hours

Distance: 1.3-mile loop with cross connector trail forming .25-mile and 1.1-mile loops

Difficulty: Easy

Blazes: None

Terrain: Level and rolling, with gradual inclines and declines

Elevation change: Approximately 40 feet

Trail conditions: Trail clearly established and well maintained, with bridges over small stream crossings

Highlights: Phenomenal old-growth forest, with massive hemlock, pine, and beech trees

Directions: From Warren along US 6, get off at the Mohawk Avenue exit (there is a sign for Hearts Content Scenic Area) and proceed south. Bear right onto Pleasant Drive (SR 3005) and follow for 11.5 miles. Bear left onto SR 2002 and follow for 3.7 miles to Hearts Content on the left. From Tidioute, follow SR 3005 for 12 miles to SR 2002 and turn right.

Some trails are known for their waterfalls or vistas. Hearts Content is known for its amazingly beautiful old-growth forest. It is hard to imagine that a forest of this diversity and size once existed across much of the ANF and Pennsylvania. A 20-acre parcel containing the virgin forest was donated to the USDA Forest Service by the Wheeler and Dusenbury Lumber Company in 1922. The scenic area now covers 120 acres. This is an ideal trail for children.

From the parking area, the trail begins at a sign for the scenic area. Pass a display showing the bark of different trees, and bear left onto the loop. Enter a mature forest with hemlocks and hardwoods. Descend slightly to a second display, about deer and their effect on the forest. The cross connector joins from the right and creates a .25-mile short loop. Continue straight on the main trail and descend slightly to the heart of the virgin forest, where massive pine, hemlock, and beech trees rise over 100 feet. The trunks of some of these trees are impressive. Another feature is the silvery, straight trunks of dead pine trees. Look around the forest floor and notice the plant life and number of large fallen logs. Old-growth forests are characterized not only by the size of the living trees, but also the dead trees that lie on the ground.

Dead trees decompose, replenish the soil, and provide nourishment for the next generation, along with habitat for numerous species of plants and animals.

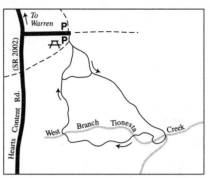

Pass a plaque to the Wheeler and Dusenbury Lumber Company near a seep spring. Cross a log bridge over a small stream. The trail recrosses the stream over another bridge underneath deep hemlocks. Cross the stream yet again, and gradually climb along the trail. Bear

Hike 22: Hearts Content National Scenic Area

right, pass the headwaters of West Branch Tionesta Creek, and reach a small deer fence enclosure. A side trail to the left goes to the picnic area and field. The trail to the right is the cross connector trail. Proceed straight to complete the loop.

🚶🚶 23. Tom's Run and Ironwood Loops

Duration: 2 to 3 hours

Distance: 4.1-mile loop

Difficulty: Easy

Blazes: Blue; Tanbark Trail is blazed with white/gray diamonds

Terrain: Level and rolling, with gradual ascents and descents

Elevation change: 200 feet

Trail conditions: Trails are well established and blazed, with bridges over several small stream crossings

Highlights: Deep hemlock forests, scenic streams, isolation

Directions: From Warren along US 6, get off at the Mohawk Avenue exit (there is a sign for Hearts Content Scenic Area) and proceed south. Bear right onto Pleasant Drive (SR 3005) and follow for 11.5 miles. Bear left onto SR 2002 and follow for 3.7 miles to Hearts Content on the left. From Tidioute, follow SR 3005 for 12 miles to SR 2002 and turn right.

These trails are also known as the Hearts Content Cross-Country Ski Trails. Both loops are easy and offer similar scenery. This hike combines parts of the two loops for a total of 4.1 miles.

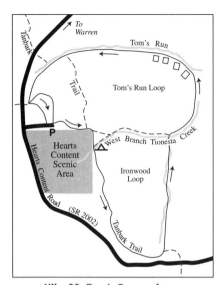

Hike 23: Tom's Run and Ironwood Loops

From the parking area, follow the trail for Tom's Run Loop; the Hearts Content Scenic Interpretive Trail is to your right. The trail follows level terrain through a diverse forest of hemlocks, pines, and hardwoods. Begin a gradual descent along a seasonal stream. After .5 mile, turn right onto the Tanbark Trail to begin the Ironwood Loop. The Tom's Run Loop continues straight. The Tanbark Trail is less established but still easy to follow. Gradually descend to a small stream with a campsite and beautiful hemlocks. This stream is West Branch Tionesta Creek. A blue-blazed side trail descends along the creek to your left.

Cross the stream and begin a long, gradual ascent back up to the plateau. The top has rolling terrain, with meadows and forests of hardwoods and deep hemlocks. Sections of this trail are curvy, so keep a close eye on the blazes. Begin a gradual descent and turn left onto the blue-blazed Ironwood Loop; the Tanbark Trail continues on to the right.

The trail now descends gradually along an old grade down a stream valley. Pass through hemlocks, then a large meadow, and reenter a long tunnel of hemlocks. A small stream flows to the left. Pass along more meadows. An unestablished side trail blazed white leads to Dunham Siding. Cross the creek twice and continue gradual descent; notice the railroad ties still embedded in the grade. In a meadow, continue straight on Tom's Run Loop, which the trail rejoins.

The trail now follows a level grade through hemlocks and hardwoods. The hardwoods begin to dominate the forest as you pass a few boulders. The trail maintains its elevation above the stream valley off to your right. As the trail curves to the left and enters another stream valley, hemlocks become more common. Pass an unblazed, unmarked side trail to the right that leads to Chapman Dam State Park. Begin a gradual ascent through thick hemlocks. Boulders and outcrops also become more common along the trail. The stream to the right has small cascades and flows through a valley darkened by hemlocks and pines. Hike through a meadow and reenter the forest; continue the gradual ascent. The trail never crosses the stream but does cross small springs that flow from the left. Hike across another meadow with blowdowns.

Reenter the forest and reach a juncture with the Tanbark Trail. This trail follows Tom's Run Loop for a short distance before leaving to the right. Reach Hearts Content Road to the right. The trail does not cross the road, but turns left along a pine plantation. Circumvent the plantation and turn right; the trail passes a logging display and returns to the parking area.

24. Tidioute Overlook

Duration: ½ hour

Distance: .3 mile

Difficulty: Easy

Blazes: None

Terrain: Level with gradual declines and inclines

Elevation change: 20 feet

Trail conditions: Trail is well established

Highlights: Views of the Allegheny River and Tidioute

Directions: From the juncture of SR 3005 and US 62 near Tidioute, follow SR 3005 for 1.2 miles. Turn left into the parking area.

This small triangular loop features two vistas: River and Town Overlooks. Begin by hiking a short distance underneath hemlocks to the impressive River Overlook. Beneath you is Courson Island, one of seven islands in the Allegheny River Islands Wilderness. The overlook is about 500 feet above the river and provides a nice, bucolic view of a narrow val-

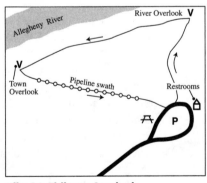

Hike 24: Tidioute Overlook

ley surrounded by steep plateaus. The river stretches off into the distance, studded with islands.

Follow the trail gradually uphill along the edge of the plateau. To the right, the slope drops steeply and is home to hemlocks. Reach Town Overlook, a partially overgrown view of Tidioute and the hills to the west. Follow the trail along a pipeline swath downhill back to the parking area.

25. East Hickory Creek

Duration: 1 to 2 hours

Distance: .8 mile (one-way)

Difficulty: Moderate

Blazes: White/gray diamonds

Terrain: Rolling with gradual descents; one steep section through a crevasse

Elevation change: 150 feet

Trail conditions: Trail is well blazed and maintained

Highlights: Tanbark Trail, East Hickory Creek, massive cliffs, boulders, and outcrops.

Directions: From Warren along US 6, get off at the Mohawk Avenue exit (there is a sign for Hearts Content Scenic Area) and proceed south. Bear right onto Pleasant Drive (SR 3005) and follow for 11.5 miles. Bear left onto SR 2002 and follow for 3.2 miles to a pull-off on the right; there is a sign for the Tanbark Trail. From Tidioute, follow SR 3005 for 12 miles to SR 2002 and turn right.

This hike is one of the most scenic sections of the 9-mile linear Tanbark. From the road, hike along the Tanbark Trail north as it gradually ascends under hardwoods. After reaching the crest, descend more steeply. The trail turns right and gradually descends to a flat area above cliffs. Turn left and descend steeply through a crevasse between the cliffs and boulders. Upon leaving the crevasse, you are immediately faced with a huge boulder that has hemlocks growing on top. The trail bends to the right and gradually descends into the valley of East Hickory Creek, passing car-size boulders.

As you near the bottom of the valley, hemlocks become more common. Cross a bridge over small, scenic East Hickory Creek, a good trout stream with a the bed of gravel and sand. Campsites are off to the left. The trail gradually ascends under a hardwood forest; notice how the forest changes on the south-facing slopes. Pass car-size boulders, and two large boulders to the right. Continue the gradual ascent until you reach the trail's highlights—a massive overhanging cliff and a monstrous, house-size boulder to the right. It is possible to camp under the cliff; the boulder is probably 40 to 50 feet high. More large boulders lie downslope. This is a fascinating place to explore. From here, retrace your steps.

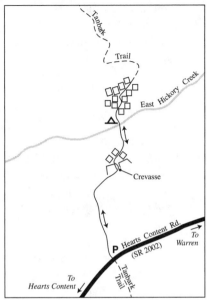

Hike 25: East Hickory Creek

26. Buckaloons Seneca Interpretive Trail

Duration: 1 hour

Distance: 1-mile loop

Difficulty: Easy

Blazes: None

Terrain: Rolling with minimal change in elevation

Elevation change: 10 feet

Trail conditions: Trail is well established and maintained

Highlights: Irvine Run, Brokenstraw Creek, Allegheny River, Buckaloons Recreation Area, history, sizable trees, diverse vegetation

Directions: From the intersection of US 6 and US 62 (6 miles west of Warren), proceed south on US 62 for .4 mile. Turn right onto SR 3022, follow for .2 mile, and turn left into the Buckaloons Recreation Area. Drive to the parking area near the boat launch and restrooms. There is a fee to use the recreation area.

This easy trail is ideal for children. It is educational in that it illustrates the relationship between a river and its tributaries. In quick succession, you hike along the Allegheny River; Brokenstraw Creek, a primary tributary; and Irvine Run, a secondary tributary.

Because this loop is located at the juncture of the river and its tributaries, the fertile riparian soils support diverse, thick vegetation that resembles a verdant rain forest in summer. The recreation area offers diverse vegetation, with shagbark hickory, oak, silver maple, sycamore, hawthorne, white pine, and locust trees, some of them truly massive.

This loop trail is also historic. Buckaloons was a Seneca Indian village for thousands of years before being destroyed by General Brodhead in 1779. Burial mounds discovered here indicate that Buckaloons had been inhabited for 20,000 years.

Begin by following the cindered trail to the right of the boat launch. Proceed downstream along the Allegheny River. Pass picnic areas, open fields, and parking areas to your right. Reach a bench at the juncture of Brokenstraw Creek and the river. Proceed upstream along Brokenstraw Creek. This large stream with massive sycamores is ideal for fishing or wading when the water is low, and it can be canoed in the spring.

The trail soon bears right and proceeds upstream along small Irvine Run, a clear mountain stream. Notice how parts of the run are crowded with Japanese knotweed, an invasive species. The trail moves a little way from the run and climbs gently to a grove of scenic hemlocks and large white pines. Begin to bear right as the trail curves around the north end of the loop, near Irvine Road (SR 3022) and the recreation area's access road. Follow the trail between the access road and a camping area. Cross a road and return to the parking lot.

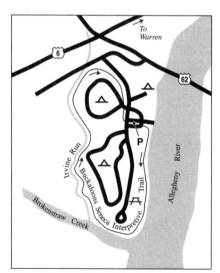

Buckaloons Recreation Area also offers a scenic campground with picnic sites, playing fields, and great opportunities for fishing.

**Hike 26: Buckaloons Seneca
Interpretive Trail**

Allegheny National Forest: Marienville Ranger District

The Marienville Ranger District encompasses the southern half of the national forest. Elevations are not as high as those found farther north, and the terrain is more moderate. The trails in this district feature beautiful streams and rivers and many opportunities to view wildlife. This section also includes a few bushwhacks that reveal the ANF's hidden gems.

Contact information: Marienville Ranger District, Star Route 2, Box 130, Marienville, PA 16239; phone: 814-927-6628. Allegheny National Forest, PO Box 847, Warren, PA 16365; phone: 814-723-5150; websites: www.fs. fed.us/r9/forests/allegheny/ and www.allegheny-online.com/hiking trails.html.

27. Black Cherry National Recreational Interpretive Trail

Duration: 1 hour

Distance: 1.4-mile double loop

Difficulty: Easy

Blazes: Gray/white

Terrain: Level and rolling

Elevation change: 180 feet

Trail conditions: Trail is well established and blazed

Highlights: Interpretive trail, Twin Lakes Trail, scenic forest

Directions: The trail is at the Twin Lakes Recreation Area. From Kane, drive 6.1 miles south on PA 321. Turn right and follow FR 191 2 miles to the campground area. The trail begins a few hundred feet along a gated road, straight ahead from the entrance road. From Wilcox, proceed north for 3 miles along PA 321.

This short trail is composed of two loops that encircle a campground in the Twin Lakes Recreation Area. One loop is a mile; the shorter loop is .4 mile. This trail is also the eastern end of the Twin Lakes Trail and features thirty-six interpretive stops.

The trail explores the valley of a small stream. The surrounding forest is typical of the region, with black cherry, ash, beech, birch, maple, and some hemlock trees. The understory consists of ferns, witch hazel, and ironwood.

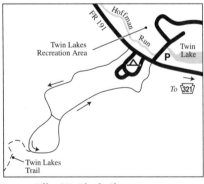

Hike 27: Black Cherry National Recreational Interpretive Trail

From the campground, walk up FR 191 a short distance and turn left to begin the trail. Gradually ascend the valley until the trail bears left and crosses a small seasonal stream. Reach the beginning of the small loop, bear right and hike up the valley where the trail joins with the Twin Lakes Trail. At this juncture, turn left and descend on the opposite side of the valley, returning to FR 191 and the campground.

👣 28. Mill Creek Trail

Duration: 1 to 2 hours

Distance: 1.2 mile (one-way)

Difficulty: Easy

Blazes: Gray/white

Terrain: Flat

Elevation change: 100 feet

Trail conditions: The trail is brushy in sections, with blazes infrequent in places

Highlights: Big Mill Creek, pine plantations, hemlocks, spruce trees

Directions: From Ridgway, follow PA 948 for 10.5 miles north, to a sign and parking area on the right

The 5.6-mile linear Mill Creek Trail connects the Twin Lakes Trail and PA 948. The northern section of the trail has suffered from blowdowns and maintenance problems, so this hike explores the southern part of the trail, which is also considered to be more scenic. This is an easy trail, but it is brushy in sections. This hike follows an old grade up the Big Mill Creek Valley.

From the parking area, follow the grade for .1 mile and turn right at a juncture with the Brush Hollow trail system. Descend and cross a bridge over Big Mill Creek. This is a scenic spot, as the creek meanders through a hemlock forest downstream. Turn left and follow the grade. Big Mill Creek is to your left for a short distance but soon meanders out of sight. The trail does not follow the creek.

After .2 mile, pass between a pine plantation on the left and thick spruce trees on the right. The trail enters an open hardwood forest; cross a bridge over a small stream after .4 mile from the pine plantation. You enter an area of thick blowdowns .2 mile farther, but the trail has been cleared through the fallen trees. Most of the trees appear to be black cherry.

Continue along the grade through a hardwood forest. Prior to reaching another pine plantation, the trail is soggy. Pass along the plantation with spruce and hemlocks. Enter a hardwood forest and another pine plantation. This hike ends at a narrow pipeline swath. Return the way you came.

Hike 28: Mill Creek Trail
Hike 29: Brush Hollow Trail

🚶🚶 29. Brush Hollow Trail

Duration: 2½ to 3 hours

Distance: 3.75-mile loop

Difficulty: Moderate

Blazes: Blue

Terrain: Rolling with gradual inclines and declines

Elevation change: 275 feet

Trail conditions: Trails are well established; blazes are infrequent, but there are signs at every trail juncture

Highlights: Big Mill Creek, Ellithorpe Run, hemlock forests, vista

Directions: From Ridgway, follow PA 948 for 10.5 miles north, to a sign and parking area on the right

Brush Hollow is a cross-country ski trail system that is also open to hiking. The system is composed of three loops: Elli, Brushy Gap, and Challenger Loops. This hike follows the Brushy Gap and Challenger Loops along streams and through hemlock and hardwood forests. This is a scenic and enjoyable trail, with a nice vista near the end of the hike.

From the parking area, follow the grade and pass a juncture with the Mill Creek Trail after .1 mile. Continue straight on the grade for .3 mile, closely following scenic Big Mill Creek through a hemlock forest. Reach a juncture with Challenger Loop; proceed straight and cross Brush Hollow Run. Reach a juncture with Brushy Gap Loop with moderate-size boulders to the left. Proceed straight on the grade, following Big Mill Creek upstream through a hemlock forest. The creek flows in and out of sight of the trail. Cross two bridges over wet areas. After .6 mile, reach a juncture with Elli Loop. A beautiful place to take a rest is the bridge over Ellithorpe Run, just ahead. However, this hike follows Brushy Gap Loop to the left. You can extend your hike by including Elli Loop, which primarily explores an open hardwood forest.

Follow another grade up the stream valley of Ellithorpe Run, through a hemlock and hardwood forest. The run itself is out of sight. After .4 mile, the run meanders in sight before the trail enters a hardwood forest. Bear left and reach a juncture with the Elli Loop. Continue straight and follow the Brushy Gap Loop as it climbs along a small stream through an open hardwood forest. This is a gradual, 100-vertical-foot climb. Reach a pump and forest road to the right. The trail bends left, then right, and continues a gradual climb. Notice how the forest to the left is filled with saplings and young trees. The trail descends gradually and reaches a juncture with the Challenger Loop; follow the trail to the right.

Descend to the small Brush Hollow Run and cross a bridge. Begin a slight ascent and turn left. For the next mile, the trail follows rolling terrain along the contour of the plateau. The Challenger Loop is not a wide grade and looks like a more typical hiking trail. The hardwood forest dominates, but there are occasional groves of hemlocks, some of impressive size. The trail turns sharply to the left and passes a nice vista overlooking the Big Mill Creek valley to the north. Continue the descent to the valley and turn sharply to the right to complete the loop. Follow the trail to the right to return to the parking area.

30. Hemlock and Scout Loops (Laurel Mill Trail)

Duration: 2 to 3 hours

Distance: 4.6-mile loop

Difficulty: Moderate

Blazes: Blue

Terrain: Level and rolling, with gradual ascents and descents

Elevation change: 300 feet

Trail conditions: Trails are well established but wet in areas; blazes are infrequent in places, but all trail junctures have signs

Highlights: Big Mill Creek, Ridgway Reservoir, beautiful hemlock forests

Directions: From Ridgway, follow Laurel Mill Road (SR 3002) for 3.6 miles. Sign and large parking area are on the right.

The Laurel Mill Trail system comprises several loops and connector trails that total 11.6 miles. The trails are open to both hiking and cross-country skiing; the latter is very popular in winter. Please do not hike in the ski tracks. This hike is the more scenic of the two described along the Laurel Mill Trail.

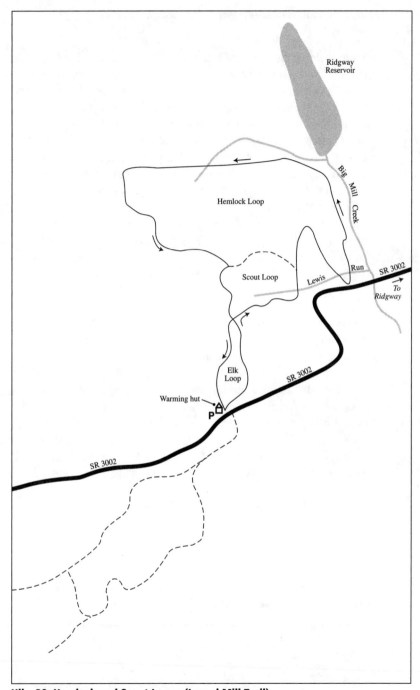

Hike 30: Hemlock and Scout Loops (Laurel Mill Trail)

From the parking area, walk to the trail sign and warming hut; the trail begins to the left along the Elk Loop. It descends gradually through an open hardwood forest, bears left and crosses a small stream, and follows rolling terrain until reaching the Scout Loop. Make a sharp right onto this loop and follow the trail as it forms a boundary between a hemlock forest to the left and a hardwood forest to the right. The trail steepens along a grade and is wet in many places as it descends into a glen with a mixture of hemlock and hardwood trees. Turn left and cross a bridge over the small Lewis Run. Ascend slightly and reach a juncture with the Hemlock Loop.

Turn right and descend along the grade as it winds down the plateau. The trail veers right and enters an impressive hemlock forest. Turn left onto another grade at the bottom of the valley; SR 3002 is just to the right. For the next .7 mile, the trail follows a grade up the Big Mill Creek valley; the creek itself is usually out of sight. Much of this trail is surrounded by a beautiful hemlock forest. The trail turns left and ascends; the Ridgway Reservoir is off to the right and can be seen through the trees. As you ascend, the forest changes back to an open hardwood forest and will remain that way until you reach the Scout Loop again.

Continue the ascent until the trail levels off on top of the plateau. Cross a small stream and continue a gentle climb along rolling terrain. The trail makes a sudden left and leaves the grade, or old swath. An electric line is off to the right. The trail is rolling for the next .9 mile, until it reaches the Scout Loop. Bear right onto the Scout Loop, and the trail soon enters a deep, verdant hemlock and spruce forest that is very scenic. The trail returns you to the Elk Loop, on which you turn right. Follow the trail for .6 mile as it gradually ascends and ends near the restrooms. The parking area is to the right.

31. Perseverance and Sparrow Nest Loops (Laurel Mill Trail)

Duration: 3 to 4 hours

Distance: 5.4-mile loop

Difficulty: Easy

Blazes: Blue

Terrain: Level and rolling
Elevation change: 100 feet
Trail conditions: Trails usually follow old grades and are established, although sections of Sparrow Nest Loop are less established. Blazes may be infrequent, but all trail junctures have signs.
Highlights: Isolation, hardwood forests
Directions: From Ridgway, follow Laurel Mill Road (SR 3002) for 3.6 miles, to the sign and large parking area on the right

This hike does not have many scenic features, although it does offer a lot of isolation as it explores a roadless and undeveloped area above the Clarion River. The forest is composed almost exclusively of open hardwoods. You also pass through two small meadows and a small grove of pines and hemlocks. The terrain is level and rolling, without any difficult ascents or descents.

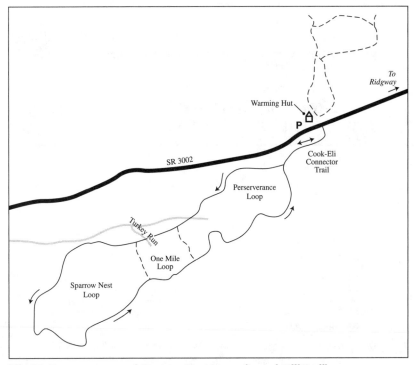

Hike 31: Perseverance and Sparrow Nest Loops (Laurel Mill Trail)

From the parking area, go to the trail sign and cross SR 3002 to begin the hike along the Cook-Eli Connector Trail. This .4-mile trail crosses a small stream and reaches Perseverance Loop. Turn right on the loop, and after .8 mile, cross a small stream and reach a juncture with One Mile Loop. Turn right and begin a slight descent, crossing small seasonal streams, including Turkey Run. Reach a juncture and go straight onto Sparrow Nest Loop. The trail continues to follow an old grade as it descends into a stream valley. It then leaves the grade and ascends slightly to the left. Unlike the other loops, much of Sparrow Nest does not follow a grade; it is also not as well established as the others. Pass an area called Lunch Rocks on the map, although I didn't see any rock outcrops when I hiked this trail. After .8 mile, cross a small meadow that is a popular place for wild turkeys. Follow the trail as it meanders and descends to a small grove of pines and hemlocks. Off to the right is a large meadow.

Begin a gradual ascent, and after .5 mile, bear right onto One Mile Loop. Descend gradually and reach a juncture with Perseverance Loop. Bear right onto this trail as it meanders through the forest. After .6 mile, pass through a small meadow along a gradual ascent. The remaining .6 mile of this loop descends along an old grade back to the Cook-Eli Connector Trail. Return the way you came.

32. Little Drummer Historical Pathway

Duration: 2 to 3 hours

Distance: 3.1-mile double loop

Difficulty: Easy

Blazes: Gray/white

Terrain: Level and rolling

Elevation change: 60 feet

Trail conditions: Trail is well established and blazed, although many sections are wet

Highlights: History, spruce plantations, diverse habitats, Cole Run Pond, wetlands, wildlife watching

Directions: From Ridgway, follow Laurel Mill Road (SR 3002) for 8.3 miles, to a sign and parking area on the right

Named after the grouse that live here, commonly known as drummers, this trail is one of the finest in the forest, featuring diverse habitats, forty interpretive stops, and excellent opportunities for wildlife- and bird-watching. It is also historic, as it follows old railroad grades, pipelines, and abandoned sites of Civilian Conservation Corps camps from the 1930s. Pick up an interpretive guide so you can understand the significance of each stop. The trail consists of two loops—the shorter one a mile, the longer 2.1 miles—and is known for having many wet areas along the wetlands. When I first hiked this trail, I met a lady who proudly proclaimed that this was the most scenic trail in the national forest.

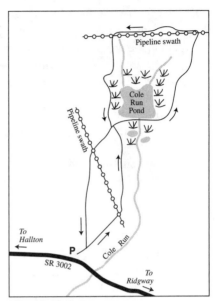

Hike 32: Little Drummer Historical Pathway

From the parking area, follow the trail past the restrooms and to the beginning of the short loop. Bear right as the trail follows an old railroad grade through a thick spruce grove. Hike along a small meadow and cross a pipeline swath. Pass through another spruce grove, followed by another meadow. The hardwood forest returns as the trail follows a long boardwalk over boggy areas. Tunnel though some saplings and reach a juncture with the longer loop. Turn right to hike the longer loop and cross over the top of the earthen dam that creates Cole Run Pond. Extensive wetlands and sedges surround the pond, and this is an excellent spot to view birds and other wildlife. More wetlands and beaver ponds lie downstream below the pond.

After crossing the dam, the trail enters the forest and bears left as it makes a slight ascent. The trail remains close to the wetlands and provides views over the pond. Hike through a stand of larch trees followed by a meadow. Turn right along an old abandoned gas-line swath, and hike up and over a small hill. After .5 mile, you reach the old railroad grade, on which the trail turns left. The swath continues straight and once supplied Ridgway with gas; it was hand dug by workers.

The trail continues to follows the old railroad grade as it crosses a field that was once a lumber camp. Pass through open meadows along the wetlands and pond, with lowbush blueberries and bluebird boxes. Continue along the wetlands, with views over the pond, and follow a boardwalk across boggy areas. Return to the juncture with the shorter loop.

Turn right and follow a grassy access road up a slight hill through a hardwood forest. Cross the same pipeline swath you did before, and hike along a large spruce plantation to the left. The trail descends slightly and returns you to the beginning of the short loop. Follow the short connector trail back to the parking area.

33. Clarion River Rapids

Duration: 2 to 3 hours

Distance: 2.5 miles (one-way)

Difficulty: Easy

Blazes: None

Terrain: Level; trail follows old railroad grade along the river

Elevation change: 40 feet

Trail conditions: Trail is not blazed or maintained, but it is clearly established for the first mile, after which it becomes less established, with more blow-downs and brush. It follows an old railroad grade along the river.

Highlights: Incredible scenery, Clarion River, boulders, pools, rapids, rhododendrons, isolation, campsites

Directions: From Ridgway, follow Laurel Mill Road (SR 3002) for 10.6 miles, to the Irwin Run canoe launch and parking area on the left

Despite the beautiful Clarion River's popularity as a canoe stream, there are no officially recognized or maintained trails along the river. Don't let this deter you from exploring the riverbanks. Old railroad grades, once used to transport lumber, lie along the river, hidden in the cloak of the forest. This hike follows such a grade and is one of the most beautiful hikes in the ANF, if not western Pennsylvania. It is exceptional, featuring a scenic river, large boulders and outcrops,

rapids, and verdant hemlocks and
rhododendrons in an isolated setting. It is rare to find so many
attributes along one trail.

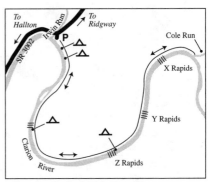

Begin by hiking upstream along
the old grade from the Irwin Run
canoe launch parking area. The
trail is obvious and clearly established. After a few hundred feet,
pass a campsite near large boulders
in the river. Soon thereafter, the
trail passes large boulders in the
river and rises to meet the railroad

Hike 33: Clarion River Rapids

grade. Follow the grade above the river; notice the island in the river.
Enter thick rhododendrons covering the grade as the trail weaves
through the foliage. The rhododendrons diminish as the trail reaches
unnamed rapids, found .7 mile from Irwin Run. By these rapids are
wooden benches and excellent camping. Large boulders lie downstream, and there is a small beach. The scenery is excellent.

Continue to hike along the trail through thick rhododendrons along
the grade. At times, the trail leaves the grade and follows the bank
above the river to the right. Pass Z Rapids, indicated by a painted "Z"
on a boulder, as the trail continues to follow along the river and not
the grade. Sections of this trail may be unestablished, but the forest is
open and the grade is nearby, so it is impossible to get lost.

After 1.5 miles from Irwin Run, the trail passes Y Rapids, with more
boulders. Continue to follow the grade through open hardwoods and
ferns. The grade has a faint trail with brush and several blowdowns.
The river flows closely to the right. After .5 mile from Y Rapids, you
reach X Rapids. The trail on the grade becomes even less established,
with blowdowns and brush, although the grade itself is clearly evident. Cross small streams and springs. The trail becomes more obvious where the grade passes through a cut behind a huge boulder
harboring rhododendrons. Reach campsites on a bench above the
river, beneath hemlocks and pines; notice the No Camping sign. The
trail ends where the grade is washed away by Cole Run.

 34. Pigeon Run Falls

Duration: 1 to 2 hours

Distance: .9 mile (one-way)

Difficulty: Easy

Blazes: None

Terrain: Level

Elevation change: 40 feet

Trail conditions: Trail is well established but not blazed

Highlights: Spring Creek, isolation, Pigeon Run Falls

Directions: From Marienville, follow East Spruce Street, which becomes FR 130 for 8.7 miles. The road crosses a narrow bridge over Spring Creek, and there is some space to park on the right. This is a dirt road passable to cars, but not if there is snow.

This is one of the most scenic trails in the ANF. The trail begins in state game lands but crosses into the national forest. Begin by hiking the old railroad grade north from FR 130; notice the small, triangular, green placards along the trail, indicating that this grade is open to horses and mountain biking. These placards are not along the trail in the national forest.

The old grade crosses Hill Run and follows level terrain along the contour of a hill above scenic Spring Creek, a large, crystal-clear stream that flows off to your left. Here the creek meanders through a wide field. You can see glimpses of this stream through the trees. The isolation of this region is impressive, with no traffic or noises from towns or highways. Even the pipes and pumps common in the ANF are absent along this trail.

The grade leaves the hardwood forest and passes through a large field, with thick spruce, hemlocks and pines off to your left. The trail is clearly established. It rises slightly as Spring Creek returns into view at the confluence of Pigeon Run. Bear right and enter Pigeon Run's glen. You can hear the stream tumbling through thick hemlocks. The grade proceeds straight, but the trail turns left and descends to beautiful Pigeon Run Falls, a 15-foot tiered waterfall that tumbles into a pool. Small cascades lie upstream. This is beautiful place to relax or camp. The stream valley is very scenic, with outcrops, hemlocks, and pines. Excellent potential campsites can also be found along Spring Creek, a fairly good freestone trout stream. The isolation and scenery of this valley invite off-trail exploration, fishing, and camping.

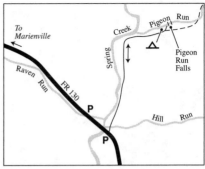

Because waterfalls are relatively rare in the ANF, especially in the southern part of the forest, this is a unique place. Please treat it with respect so that others may enjoy it too.

If you enjoy large rock cities and outcrops, you'll find such a forma-

Hike 34: Pigeon Run Falls

tion along the way to Pigeon Run Falls along FR 130. Drive 5.5 miles east from Marienville to a pull-off on the left. Massive boulders and ledges are on the hillside on the right side of the road. Some of these boulders are more than 30 feet high and the size of houses.

35. Loleta Trail

Duration: 1½ to 3 hours

Distance: 3-mile loop

Difficulty: Moderate

Blazes: White/gray diamonds

Terrain: Rolling with moderate descents and ascents

Elevation change: 200 feet

Trail conditions: Trail is well blazed and established

Highlights: Scenic streams, rock outcrops, Loleta Recreation Area

Directions: From Marienville, proceed south on South Forest Street, which becomes Loleta Road (SR 2005) for 6 miles. Turn left into the Loleta Recreation Area, and follow this road to a parking area on the left. You must pay a $5 fee. In winter the recreation area is closed; to hike the trail, park along Loleta Road.

This loop begins and ends in the Loleta Recreation Area, which features picnic areas, a small beach, and campgrounds. For those not camping, a $5 daily use fee is required to use the recreation area. The

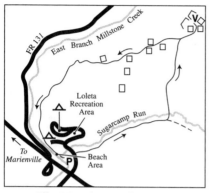

Hike 35: Loleta Trail

area is closed in the winter, but you can easily access the trail from SR 3002.

From the parking area, hike to the road. Turn right and reach the beginning of the loop to the left. The trail begins a moderate, rolling ascent up the valley of Sugarcamp Run. The valley is dominated by hardwoods, including many ironwood trees, and has a series of small meadows. After .6 mile, the trail enters a large meadow and turns left; another grade and unblazed trail proceeds straight. Descend gradually, cross Sugarcamp Run over rocks, and climb the steep bank on the other side.

Continue the gradual ascent through small meadows and occasional spruce trees. Enter a hardwood forest, and after .3 mile from Sugarcamp Run, turn right onto a grassy forest road. After .2 mile on this road, turn right onto the .2-mile spur trail that leads to the overlook. This spur trail gradually ascends through thick ground pine to reach the overlook at a rock ledge. Because of the trees, there usually isn't anything to see, but you are offered a view of the Millstone Creek valley when the leaves are off.

Return to the loop, bear right, and follow the trail as it traverses the rim of the plateau. The terrain is level and rolling, but rocky, with abundant ground pine. After .5 mile, begin a gradual descent off the plateau and pass a few moderate-size boulders. The trail is level for a short distance before making a steeper descent via switchbacks. Hike along sidehill above East Branch Millstone Creek as it gradually descends to the group camping area in the Loleta Recreation Area. Proceed straight onto a gated trail; the access road comes in from the left. Hike across a mowed field, pass the picnic area and the beach, and cross Sugarcamp Run. The parking area is to your left.

36. Songbird Sojourn Interpretive Trail

Duration: 1 hour

Distance: 1.6-mile loop

Difficulty: Easy

Blazes: White/gray diamonds

Terrain: Level and rolling

Elevation change: 120 feet

Trail conditions: Trail is fairly well blazed and established

Highlights: Interpretive trail with numbered stations

Directions: From Marienville, proceed south on South Forest Street (SR 2005) for 1.2 miles and turn left onto FR 157. Follow this road for 2.4 miles to a large parking area on the left.

This trail contains seventeen numbered stations that correspond to a trail guide. These stations offer insight into the trees, habitats, and animals of the forest. Begin by hiking the loop counterclockwise along level terrain. The trail is also blazed blue, indicating that it is also a part of the Buzzard Swamp trail system. Enter an area with spruce trees and pines; the Buzzard Swamp Trail leaves to the right.

The trail enters a grove of red pines and more spruce and descends to cross a small stream between Stations 2 and 3. Pass beech and birch trees, and the Buzzard Swamp Trail rejoins from the right. Begin a gradual ascent through a hardwood forest, passing maple trees. The Buzzard Swamp Trail leaves again to the right; continue a gradual ascent as the trail weaves uphill. Pass a large gully with a seep spring off to your right, and hike near a field that serves as a wildlife opening. Begin a gradual descent through a hardwood forest with club moss, also known as ground

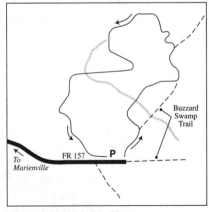

Hike 36: Songbird Sojourn Interpretive Trail

pine. Pass a seep spring at Station 11 and continue a mild descent. The trail turns right onto an old grade. Between Stations 13 and 14, cross a small stream, which flows from the seep spring near Station 11 and is the same stream you crossed between Stations 2 and 3. The trail explores a young hardwood forest and gradually descends to complete the loop.

37. Buzzard Swamp Trail

Duration: 1 1/2 to 3 hours

Distance: 4-mile loop

Difficulty: Easy

Blazes: Blue blazes are spaced far apart, but the trail follows a gated road and there are informational signs at trail junctures

Terrain: Level

Elevation change: 50 feet

Trail conditions: Trail follows a gated grassy and gravel road; expect a lot of exposure on hot, sunny days

Highlights: Wildlife viewing, views, ponds, spruce and pine forests, large open meadows and fields

Directions: From Marienville, proceed south on South Forest Street (SR 2005) for 1.2 miles and turn left onto FR 157. Follow this road for 2.4 miles to a large parking area on the left.

The Buzzard Swamp trail system is 11.2 miles, with several loop and connector trails. This hike follows the southern loop, which encircles the largest ponds and meadows; if you'd like to extend your hike, you can easily follow the trails that lie to the north. Buzzard Swamp is home to fifteen ponds that have been built to provide habitats for wildlife, making this one of the best wildlife-viewing trails in the ANF. Numerous species of waterfowl, wading birds, insects, mammals, amphibians, and reptiles call Buzzard Swamp home. The extensive fields and meadows are filled with wildflowers.

Follow the gated road near the entrance to the parking area and hike through a deep spruce forest. To the left is a 40-acre propagation

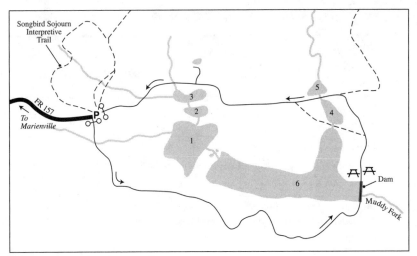

Hike 37: Buzzard Swamp Trail

area where entrance is prohibited. After .6 mile, you reach a large field with a nice view over Ponds 1, 2, and 3. Reenter the forest and pass another field that overlooks Pond 6, the largest. The trail reenters the forest yet again and then reaches a large field with an extensive view over the ponds and the wooded hills off to the west and north. Enter a hardwood forest and descend slightly to the dam that creates Pond 6; cross the top of the dam.

I hiked this trail on a blustery fall day with a strong wind as I crossed the meadows. Numerous ducks and geese were in the ponds, and several hawks flew overhead.

The road goes by picnic tables and an extensive area of meadows and fields. Pass a juncture with a grassy trail to the left; continue straight. Turn left on another gravel road and hike in front of Pond 5; Pond 4 is just below. Hike behind a wooded area and continue straight; many small fishponds are along the trail, and a large bat house is in the field near Pond 1. Turn right and pass more small fish ponds as the trail reenters the woods. Cross small streams and slightly ascend as the trail returns you to the parking area.

38. Beaver Meadows

Duration: 1 to 2½ hours

Distance: 2.8-mile loop

Difficulty: Easy

Blazes: White/gray diamonds

Terrain: Rolling and level

Elevation change: 100 feet

Trail conditions: Trail is well blazed and established

Highlights: Beaver Meadows Lake, floating boardwalk, wildlife, spruce forests

Directions: From Marienville, follow North Forest Street, which becomes Beaver Meadows Road; follow for 3.8 miles. Turn right and follow the gravel road for .9 mile to a parking area on the right.

The Beaver Meadows trail system is 6 miles long and explores wetlands, grassy savannas, and scenic forests. The main trail is the 2.5-mile Beaver Meadows Loop; you can extend your hike by including the Seldom Seen Trail, Salmon Creek Loop, or Penoke Path.

From the parking area, bear left on FR 282 and turn left to cross the top of the dam creating Beaver Meadows Lake. Enjoy views of the lake and the diverse wetland to your right. Notice the deep tea color of the water caused by decaying plants from the swamp. Cross the bridge over the spillway and climb the bank to a juncture with the Salmon Creek Loop. This 1.4-mile trail explores plantations of red pine and offers views of Salmon Creek. It climbs gradually, makes a sharp left, and descends gradually back to complete the loop.

Beaver Meadows Loop turns left and explores a forest with numerous spruce trees and an understory of ferns. Cross a small stream and reach the Lakeside Loop, a .2-mile trail that offers some views of the lake. Portions of this short trail are overgrown with ferns. Continue along the trail to a juncture with the Penoke Path. This trail is .8 mile long and features a hardwood forest. It follows an old grade along the grassy savannas and wetlands along Penoke Run.

Follow the Beaver Meadows Loop .4 mile to a glade and blueberry bushes and past the other juncture with Penoke Path. The scenery is similar to that in the beautiful Black Moshannon State Park in central Pennsylvania. Cross a long, floating boardwalk across the wetlands.

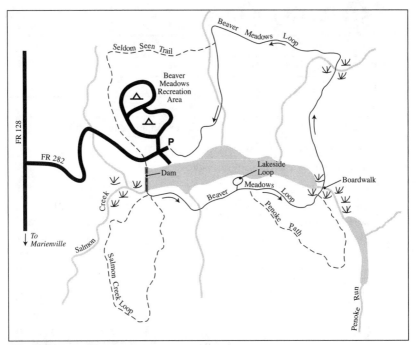

Hike 38: Beaver Meadows

Don't be surprised if your feet get wet along the boardwalk. This is an ideal place to view wildlife, especially birds.

The trail then gradually ascends through bushes and enters a mixed forest of spruce, hemlocks, and hardwoods. After .7 mile, the trail turns left and passes through a large fern meadow. Reenter the forest to the right and cross a small stream under hemlocks. The trail gradually ascends again. After .6 mile, it descends slightly to a juncture with the Seldom Seen Trail to the right along an old railroad grade. The Seldom Seen Trail is a mile long and offers scenery similar to that of the Beaver Meadows Loop, as well as fenced blueberry bushes covering half an acre. Hikers can enjoy the berries.

Continue along the Beaver Meadows Loop as it descends gradually along the railroad grade. To the right is a small stream. After .3 mile, turn right and descend from the grade. Cross the small stream. The trail winds through the forest and passes near the lake, but it does not offer much of a view. Ascend gradually underneath large white pines back to the parking area.

🚶🚶 39. Logan Falls

Duration: ½ to 1 hour

Distance: .4 mile (one-way)

Difficulty: Moderate

Blazes: White

Terrain: Descent is gradual, with a steep section at the beginning

Elevation change: 150 feet

Trail conditions: Trail is clearly established

Highlights: Logan Falls, massive boulders and outcrops, Logan Run

Directions: From the juncture of Blue Jay Road (SR 1003) and PA 666 near Lynch, cross the bridge over Tionesta Creek and follow Blue Jay Road for 1.2 miles. Make a very sharp right onto Job Corps Road (FR 128) and follow as the road ascends the mountain. After 5.2 miles, reach an intersection of five roads, known as Deadman Corners. Bear right onto FR 180 and follow for 2.5 miles to a small, grassy pull-off on the right. There is no trail sign.

aka Coal Bed Run Rd

This short trail leads to the scenic Logan Falls. From the road, descend along the clearly evident trail. The descent initially is steep but becomes more gradual. Notice the massive boulders and rock outcrops off to your left. The trail is blazed fairly well with white spray paint. It curves to the left, crosses a small meadow, and then continues a gradual descent, passing more meadows off to the right.

The trail bends left and reaches the steep bank above Logan Falls. Descend steeply along the bank to view the beautiful falls, which drop 10 feet over a ledge into a shallow pool. Although the falls are not very high, the scenery is augmented by the isolation of Logan Run, a clear mountain stream. This is a beautiful stream valley with hemlocks, boulders, and small cascades. Return the way you came.

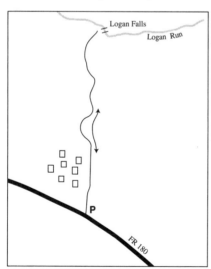

Hike 39: Logan Falls

Chapman State Park

This 805-acre park, situated in an isolated, forested valley drained by several small streams, is almost completely surrounded by the national forest and state game lands. It features a 68-acre lake, 12 miles of trails, and a campground. Hikers and backpackers enjoy using this park as a trailhead to explore trails in the surrounding national forest and game lands, particularly along an old forest road that proceeds south across State Game Lands 29 and ends near Dunham Siding. For a longer trek, all of the trails described in this section can be linked together by hiking along the park roads.

Directions: From Warren, proceed 4 miles on US 6 east to Clarendon. At the traffic light, turn right on Railroad Street (SR 2006) and drive 5 miles to the park.

Contact information: Chapman State Park, RR 2 Box 1610, Clarendon, PA 16313; phone: 814-723-0250; website: www.dcnr.state.pa.us/stateparks/parks/chapman.aspx; e-mail: chapmansp@state.pa.us

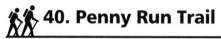

40. Penny Run Trail

Duration: 1½ hours

Distance: 1.5-mile loop

Difficulty: Easy to moderate

Blazes: Blue

Terrain: Gradual ascents and descents

Elevation change: 250 feet

Trail conditions: Trail is well established and blazed, with several small stream and spring crossings

Highlights: Beautiful hemlock forest, small streams, springs

Directions: Upon entering the park and passing the park office, turn left onto the park road that accesses the beach, camping, and picnic areas. Turn right into a large parking area for Picnic Pavilions 2 and 3.

The Penny Run Trail is probably the most scenic in the state park. About half of the trail is in the national forest. The trail features a beautiful hemlock forest with small streams that provides a cool hike even on a hot summer day. In decades to come, this forest may mature into a remarkable old-growth forest, similar to Hearts Content.

From the parking area for Picnic Pavilions 2 and 3, cross the park road and begin to hike the trail. Enter a mixed hardwood and hemlock forest along level terrain. Penny Run is hidden in a glen off to your left. Hemlocks soon begin to predominate as the trail gradually ascends along an old grade. Some trees are sizable, as they grow in the moist soil thanks to the numerous springs that flow down this glen. The trail makes an abrupt left and is level as it follows the contour of the glen. Cross several bridges and boardwalks across springs and small rivulets that feed into Penny Run.

The trail makes another left as it passes through an open hardwood forest with ferns, common in this region. Descend gradually along the side of the glen underneath more hemlocks. Pass through an area with saplings, and the trail returns you to the park road; turn left to return to the parking area.

🥾 41. Hunters Ridge Trail

Duration: 2 to 3 hours

Distance: 3-mile loop

Difficulty: Easy to moderate

Blazes: Hunters Ridge Trail is blazed orange; Warming Hut Trail is blazed red and white

Terrain: Hike begins with a moderate climb; trail often follows old grades with wet areas

Elevation change: 300 feet

Trail conditions: Trail is well blazed, although sections are not well established

Highlights: Pine plantation, hemlocks, Adams Run, Chapman Lake, a few boulders

Directions: Upon entering the park, park at the park office on the right

The Hunters Ridge Trail is the longest and most difficult at Chapman State Park. Together with the Warming Hut Trail, an enjoyable 3-mile loop is formed. Access roads to oil wells cross the trail at numerous junctures; make sure to stay on the trail. From the park office, hike up the dirt forestry road for a short distance. Bear right and enter a pine plantation. Hike up through rows of trees and pass through a meadow. Enter a grove of hemlocks and spruce, and then hike through another meadow.

Cross the same forestry road and enter a forest dominated by hemlocks. After the trail leaves the hemlocks, the climb steepens through a hardwood forest with ferns. Sections of this trail are boggy and not well established. Continue to climb through ferns and grass. At the top of the ascent, turn left onto a wide, grassy grade. Notice the boulders to your right. From here, the terrain is level or rolling along this old grade; the forest is mostly hardwoods with ferns. Follow the contour of the plateau above Chapman Lake. Keep an eye out where the trail makes a sharp right but an obvious grade joins from the left.

Begin a gradual descent through a boggy area. Cross another access road and descend gradually toward Adams Run. Cross this small run over a bridge and turn left. The Adams Run Trail continues to the right; you can extend your hike by exploring this trail, which offers

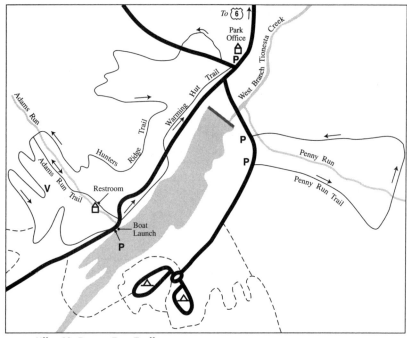

Hike 40: Penny Run Trail
Hike 41: Hunters Ridge Trail
Hike 42: Adams Run Trail

similar scenery. Hike downstream along the run. In the valley you'll find meadows and large hardwoods. Cross a bridge and pass side trails to the organized camping area. Enter a large field and picnic area with restrooms along the lake.

Turn left onto the paved park road and hike a short distance, until you bear right off the road along the Warming Hut Trail. This scenic trail follows the shore underneath hemlocks; the park road is a short distance to your left. There are many views of the lake through the forest. The trail then turns left, crosses the park road, and ascends a hill. Pass above an excavation pit and park maintenance area, and descend into a meadow with bluebird boxes. The park office is just ahead.

🥾 42. Adams Run Trail

Duration: 1 to 2 hours

Distance: 1.6-mile loop

Difficulty: Moderate

Blazes: Yellow

Terrain: Gradual descents and ascents, with a few steeper sections

Elevation change: 350 feet

Trail conditions: Trail is well blazed and mostly established; some sections are brushy

Highlights: Meadows, spruce and pine plantations, partial view

Directions: Upon entering the park, continue straight for .7 mile to a large gravel parking area on the left near a fishing pier, picnic area, and sledding hill

The Adams Run Trail is a 1.6-mile loop; about .5 mile of the loop is also a part of the Hunters Ridge Trail along Adams Run. The Hunters Ridge Trail can be used to extend this hike and offers similar scenery.

From the picnic area and boat launch, hike along the dirt road past the restrooms. Enter the woods; Adams Run is off to your left. Pass side trails to the left that lead to the organized camping area, and cross a bridge over the run. The terrain is flat, and the valley is home to hardwoods and meadows of ferns. Reach the juncture with the Hunters Run Trail to the right; proceed straight on the Adams Run Trail. Begin a winding ascent up the side of the plateau through a hardwood forest with ferns. Sections of this trail are brushy and unestablished. It switchbacks along a gradual ascent past an oil pump and meadow.

The trail then levels off and follows a grade along the contour of the plateau. When you reach a bench with a partial view of the valley, the Adams Run Trail leaves to the right and descends to the game land road. Bear left and follow the cutoff trail that is blazed yellow and red. This trail descends more steeply along switchbacks. It passes through a meadow, spruce plantation, field, and pine forest before reaching the parking area. Turn left to return to the picnic area and your car.

Cook Forest State Park

Cook Forest is one of Pennsylvania's premier state parks, offering beautiful streams, views, the Clarion River, and its greatest highlight, several tracts of old-growth forests. This 8,500-acre park has a total of 29 miles of trail and is bisected by the North Country and Baker Trails. Some of the most scenic trails in western Pennsylvania are located in Cook Forest. It is hard not to be impressed by the beauty of this park. The peaceful Clarion River bends along steep hillsides as white pines tower over the forest, offering a glimpse of what the state's forests looked like before being clear-cut.

This is the first state park in Pennsylvania specifically created to preserve a natural landmark, the old-growth and virgin forests. The forests in the park were owned by the Cook family. In the 1920s, the Cook Forest Association was formed to preserve the forests. Thanks to support from the state government and the Cook family, the forests were preserved and the park was formed. Because of their foresight, this remarkable forest and park have been enjoyed by subsequent generations.

Directions: From I-80, take Exit 78 and follow PA 36 north for 17 miles. After crossing the Clarion River, turn right to the park office.

Contact information: Cook Forest State Park, PO Box 120, Cooksburg, PA 16217-0120; phone: 814-744-8407; e-mail: cookforestsp@state.pa.us; website: www.dcnr.state.pa.us/stateparks/parks/cookforest.asp

🚶🚶 43. Forest Cathedral

Duration: 1 to 2 hours

Distance: 2.5-mile loop

Difficulty: Moderate

Blazes: The trails are not blazed except the North Country Trail (blue) and Baker Trail (yellow)

Terrain: Rolling and gradual descents and ascents, with some steep sections

Elevation change: 300 feet

Trail conditions: Trails are well maintained and established; all trail junctures have signs

Highlights: Spectacular old-growth forest, boulders, Toms Run, Forest Cathedral Natural Area and National Natural Landmark

Directions: This hike begins from the park office

The Forest Cathedral is the most popular area in the park, and one of the most beautiful. It is a state park natural area and a national natural landmark. The forest offers a spiritual high as the trails explore a remarkable forest of massive hemlocks, white pines, beeches, and black cherry. If you hike in the morning as the sun rises, you will see shafts of light piercing the forest, evoking the feeling of a more traditional cathedral. The Forest Cathedral's web of trails allows you to easily shorten or extend your hike or choose from a variety of routes.

From the park office parking area, hike up the road to the left to the Children's Fishing Pond. Turn right on the road to the Indian Cabin area and cross over Toms Run. Turn immediately right onto the Indian Trail and begin to climb a steep slope along wooden steps underneath hemlocks and pines. With the exception of the North Country and Baker Trails, the trails in the Forest Cathedral are not blazed.

The trail follows along the rim of a steep embankment above the Children's Fishing Pond. Turn left near a private-property line and follow an old grade as it gradually ascends underneath more pines and hemlocks. Along the way, you will pass massive boulders and outcrops, including one on the right with three boulders stacked upon each other. After .5 mile on the Indian Trail, you pass a juncture with the Joyce Kilmer Trail; continue straight on the Indian Trail. The trail begins a slight descent and passes more house-size boulders with trees growing on top. After .3 mile, you pass a juncture with the Rhododen-

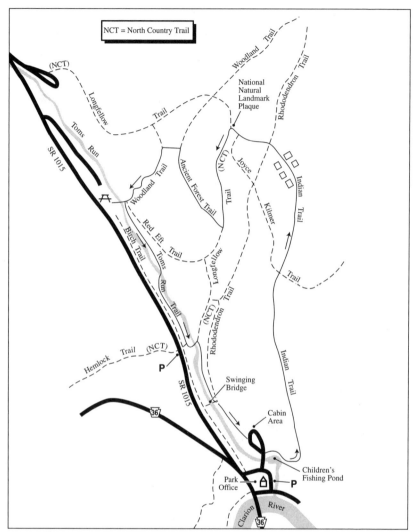

Hike 43: Forest Cathedral

dron Trail. Continue on the Indian Trail and begin a steeper descent. After .1 mile, you pass the Joyce Kilmer Trail to the left and soon thereafter reach the heart of the Forest Cathedral where the Indian Trail meets the Longfellow Trail. The North Country and Baker Trails follow the Longfellow Trail through the Forest Cathedral. Here also is a plaque indicating that the forest is a national natural landmark.

Turn left and follow the Longfellow Trail for .2 mile along a gradual descent. Turn right and follow the Ancient Forest Trail for another .2 mile. Turn left onto the Woodland Trail as it descends more steeply; avoid the trail to the right that descends into a ravine. The descent steepens until you reach Toms Run. Avoid the Red Eft Trail to the immediate left; instead, take the Toms Run Trail as it follows its namesake downstream. Do not cross the bridge. Hike downstream along the scenic run with riffles, boulders, and pools. Cross the run via a bridge and continue downstream, where you will find great scenery. Notice occasional rhododendron bushes. Cross another bridge where the North Country and Baker Trails cross. Continue downstream along the trail as it passes through meadows and glades. You can either bear left at the swinging bridge and follow a side trail a short distance to the Rhododendron Trail, turn right, and hike through the Indian Cabin area back to your car, or cross the swinging bridge and then turn left onto the Birch Trail. Upon reaching the hard road, turn left and hike back to your car.

44. Cook Trail

Duration: 1 to 2 hours

Distance: 2-mile loop

Difficulty: Moderate

Blazes: Orange/red

Terrain: Rolling and level, with mild ascents and descents

Elevation change: 400 feet

Trail conditions: Trail is well maintained and established; blazes may be infrequent

Highlights: Old-growth forest

Directions: From the park office, follow River Road for 1.2 miles to a picnic area on the left

The Cook Trail explores an old-growth forest of pines, hemlocks, and beeches. This trail has several informative signs about the forest that are very educational and interesting. From the picnic area, ascend gradually into the valley of Henry Run. The forest is composed

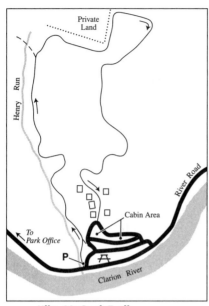

Hike 44: Cook Trail

of hardwoods and open meadows. Climb gradually out of the stream valley to the right. Pass a side trail to the right that accesses the cabin area. The trail gradually ascends and passes a dynamite shed from the Civilian Conservation Corps era and one of many fenced areas protecting the forest from deer overbrowsing. Notice the dramatic difference between the thick vegetation in the fenced area and the sparse undergrowth in the surrounding forest.

Continue a gradual ascent up the stream valley. The forest becomes dominated by large pines and hemlocks. Hike away from the stream. At a large fenced area, the trail turns left and follows the fence. Continue to hike up the valley through a scenic forest. At a juncture where the Cook Trail bears right and another trail turns left, follow the Cook Trail. This juncture is near private property. The trail steepens until it reaches the top of the plateau, where the trail is flat but very curvy. Continue to explore a deep hemlock and pine forest; the trail is often near a private-property line. After .7 mile, the trail passes the dead trunks of American chestnut trees and begins a gradual descent, with large boulders and more large trees. Reach the cabin area and follow the road to the right down to the picnic area. After .1 mile, you can also turn right on a side trail to the Cook Trail; turn left and follow the trail to your car.

45. Seneca Point and River Trail

Duration: 2 to 4 hours

Distance: 4-mile loop

Difficulty: Moderate to difficult

Blazes: Some trails are not blazed; the North Country Trail is blazed blue and the Baker Trail yellow

Terrain: Flat and rolling, with long ascents and descents that are steep in sections

Elevation change: 450 feet

Trail conditions: Trails are well established and maintained

Highlights: Old-growth forests, Seneca Point, Cook Forest Fire Tower, Clarion River, Toms Run

Directions: This hike begins from the park office

This is a particularly scenic hike that should not be missed. These trails offer a variety of features, habitats, and forest types. This is also the most difficult hike in Cook Forest.

From the park office, follow the road to PA 36, where you cross and begin hiking on the Seneca Trail. Start a gradual ascent along the steep cliffs and bank above the river. Pass a few seep springs; the terrain to the left is very steep and dangerous. The surrounding forest is typical of the state park, with hemlocks, pines, and occasional rhododendrons. After .5 mile, the Seneca Trail reaches a juncture with the North Country and Baker Trails; turn left. Hike along level terrain through thick rhododendrons and rock outcrops. At one point, the trail passes through a rock crevice. Pass behind the parking area and restrooms, and hike up an embankment to another trail juncture. Turn right to Seneca Point, featuring massive rock outcrops, boulders, crevasses, and an excellent view of the Clarion River and its meandering gorge. Return to the North Country and Baker Trails.

Hike to the Cook Forest Fire Tower, which you can climb for excellent views, especially to the east. Large rock outcrops lie below the tower. Descend the River Trail, and the North Country and Baler Trails, to the Clarion River. The descent is moderate, with several switchbacks; overall, the trail drops 400 feet in .6 mile. The forest is dominated by hardwoods, with an understory of mountain laurel. Do not

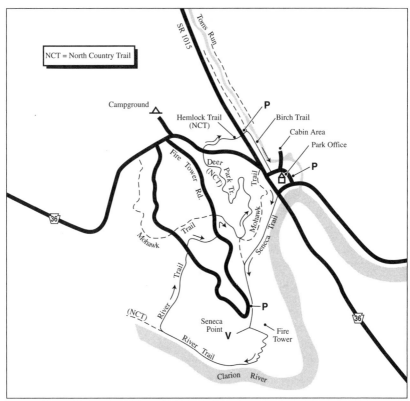

NCT = North Country Trail

Toms Run

SR 1015

Campground

Hemlock Trail (NCT)

Birch Trail

P

Cabin Area

Park Office

P

Fire Tower Rd.

Deer (NCT)

Park Tr.

Trail

P

Mohawk

Trail

Mohawk

Seneca Trail

36

Trail

River

(NCT)

Seneca Point

Fire Tower

P

36

V

River Trail

Clarion   River

Hike 45: Seneca Point and River Trail

take shortcuts across the switchbacks, because this accelerates erosion. The River Trail reaches the Clarion River in a beautiful, isolated setting, without any cottages, development, or hordes of canoeists. The opposite bank rises 500 feet above the river. Side trails lead to the river, where you can eat lunch, relax, wade, or fish. The .6-mile stretch where the River Trail follows the Clarion River is exceptionally scenic, with great views of the river and a diverse forest of hemlocks, pines, hardwoods, laurel, and rhododendrons.

At the boundary with State Game Lands 283, the North Country and Baker Trails continue straight along the river, while the River Trail turns right and begins to climb up the glen of a seasonal stream along a gated forest road. Pass a gate and continue to climb; there are a few steep sections in this 400-foot climb over .6 mile as the trail follows the gravel road past another gate and reaches Fire Tower Road. Cross the road and follow the River Trail across level terrain through a thick hemlock and pine forest for .25 mile, until the trail ends at the other side of Fire Tower Road's loop. Turn left on the road and hike it for .1 mile until the juncture with Mohawk Trail, where you turn right. Follow the trail for .2 mile to a juncture with the North Country and Baker Trails.

For a shorter hike, proceed straight on the Mohawk Trail as it descends .5 mile to PA 36. Turn right on PA 36 and hike back to the park office. Be careful hiking along the highway.

Otherwise, turn left onto the blue- and yellow-blazed North Country and Baker Trails, known here as Deer Park Trail. The trail follows the rim of the plateau, then drops down among rock outcrops. Make several curves along the trail through meadows and along boulders. The trail almost doubles back on itself and gradually climbs along boulders back to the plateau and a deep hemlock forest. Descend gradually from the plateau to PA 36. Cross the road carefully and follow the Hemlock Trail down a ravine with hemlocks and pines.

Cross SR 1015 at a parking area and turn left onto the Birch Trail. This trail initially is close to the road but then drops down along an old grade through hemlocks. Toms Run babbles below. The trail ends at a paved road. Turn left and hike down the road back to the park office.

46. Black Bear Trail

Duration: 1/2 to 1 hour	
Distance: 1-mile loop	
Difficulty: Easy	
Blazes: Orange/red	
Terrain: Level and rolling	
Elevation change: 100 feet	
Trail conditions: Trails are somewhat unestablished and poorly blazed in sections	
Highlights: Old-growth forest	
Directions: After crossing the Clarion River on PA 36 north, continue straight for .1 mile. Bear right onto SR 1015 and follow for 1.8 miles to the Sawmill Center. Turn right and drive up to the center and parking area.	

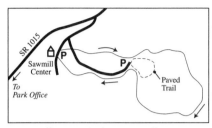

Hike 46: Black Bear Trail

The Black Bear Trail is an easy 1-mile loop that also passes a short, paved loop trail for disabled persons. From the Sawmill Center, begin the loop to the left. Hike gradually through a pine forest, and enter a mowed field with a huge blue tank off to your right. Cross a gravel road and hike across the field, along the remnants of an old road along a hedgerow, hardwood forest, and pine trees. Blazes are infrequent along this section. The trail rejoins the end of the gravel road at a parking area and the beginning of the paved loop trail.

Continue along the trail to the left as it enters a deep hemlock and pine forest and follows a loop that is somewhat unestablished and hard to follow in sections; blazes are infrequent. Reach the gravel road near the parking area again. Here the trail turns left and then right along an old grade through a thick pine forest. The tank and field are just off to your right. Descend gradually back to the Sawmill Center.

47. Deer Meadow, Browns Run, and Liggett Trails

Duration: 2 to 3 hours

Distance: 4-mile loop

Difficulty: Easy to moderate

Blazes: The trails are not blazed except the North Country Trail (blue) and Baker Trail (yellow)

Terrain: Rolling and level, with gradual descents and ascents that are often long

Elevation change: 200 feet

Trail conditions: Trails are generally well maintained and established

Highlights: Isolation, old-growth forest, Browns Run, Toms Run

Directions: After crossing the Clarion River on PA 36 north, continue straight for .1 mile. Bear right onto SR 1015 and follow for a mile to the Long Cabin Inn, Memorial Fountain, and parking area on the right.

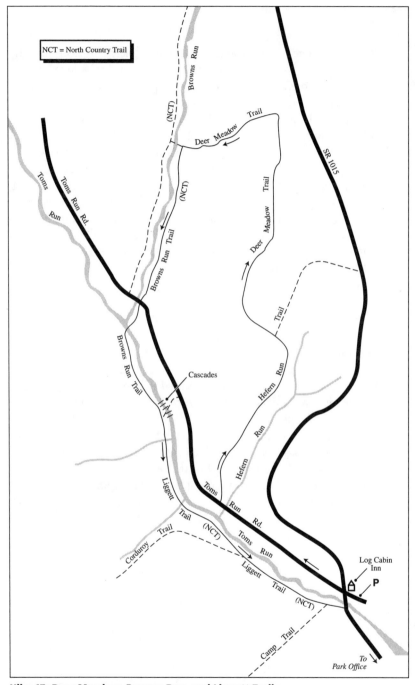

Hike 47: Deer Meadow, Browns Run, and Liggett Trails

This loop encompasses some of the most isolated areas of the park. As a result, you can expect to have these trails to yourself, unlike the trails at Forest Cathedral or Seneca Point. Browns and Toms Runs also offer backcountry trout fishing.

At the parking area, visit the Log Cabin Inn to see its interesting displays about the logging era. Cross SR 1015 and follow Toms Run Road, a single-lane dirt road, through a scenic hemlock forest. After .4 mile, turn right onto Heffern Run Trail, which follows an old forest road as it gradually ascends through a hemlock and pine forest. Off to your right, Heffern Run flows in a small glen. After .5 mile, continue straight to the Deer Meadow Trail as it ascends slightly through a mixture of hemlocks, pines, and hardwoods with small glades. The trail passes along a private-property line behind a crowded private campground. Descend gradually and turn right as the trail reaches a corner of the campground near a primitive camping area.

Follow another old grade down through a scenic forest of large trees. This descent is steeper than the climbs experienced so far on the hike. The Deer Meadow Trail ends at Browns Run Trail, which is also the North Country and Baker Trails. Turn left and follow Browns Run Trail as it follows its namesake downstream. Browns Run flows off to the right in a scenic small gorge crowded with boulders and cascades. When you reach Toms Run Road, turn right and hike along the road for a short distance before bearing left and following the trail. Cross a bridge over Toms Run and climb away from the run along another grade; the run is generally out of sight. After .3 mile, pass a bridge and trail leading to Toms Run Road to the left. Toms Run flows down a sloping rock face, creating a natural water slide. Continue straight on the Liggett Trail along the grade above Toms Run. The trail crosses wooden bridges over small side streams. The terrain is level and the forest contains more hardwoods. The Corduroy Trail joins from the right along an old grade. Continue straight and in .4 mile the Camp Trail also joins from the left. A short distance ahead is SR 1015. Turn left, cross the bridge, and return to the parking area.

Clear Creek State Park and State Forest

Despite its relatively moderate size, Clear Creek State Park is a hiking wonderland, offering 15 miles of some of the most scenic trails in this guide. The park's terrain is moderate, with a few steep sections. The hillsides are strewn with boulders and adorned with laurel and rhododendrons. Located just south of the national forest, along the beautiful Clarion River, the park also serves as a trailhead to the adjoining 9,089-acre parcels of the Clear Creek State Forest, with trails leading to the expansive vista at Beartown Rocks. The state forest offers greater isolation and lovely mountain streams that flow through tunnels of rhododendrons.

Highlights of this park are the Clarion River, views, Clear Creek, and a wealth of hiking trails. Besides hiking, the park offers camping, cabins, canoe access to the Clarion River, fishing, and hunting. Clear Creek is a good freestone trout stream. Because it exists in the shadow of the vast national forest and the more popular Cook Forest State Park, Clear Creek is one of Pennsylvania's best-kept secrets.

Directions: From I-80, take Exit 78 and follow PA 36 north for 7.4 miles to Sigel. Turn right onto PA 949 north and proceed for 4 miles to the state park and forest.

Contact information: Clear Creek State Park, 38 Clear Creek State Park Road, Sigel, PA 15860; phone: 814-752-2368; e-mail: clearcreeksp@state.pa.us; website: www.dcnr.state.pa.us/stateparks/parks/chapman.aspx. Clear Creek State Forest (a.k.a. Kittanning State Forest), 158 South Second Avenue, Clarion, PA 16214-1904; phone: 814-226-1901; website: www.dcnr.state.pa.us/forestry/stateforests/kittanning.aspx.

48. Phyllis Run Trail

Duration: ½ hour

Distance: .6-mile loop

Difficulty: Easy to moderate

Blazes: Red

Terrain: Gradual ascents and descents across rocky terrain

Elevation change: 150 feet

Trail conditions: Trail is fairly well blazed and established, although the terrain is very rocky in sections

Highlights: Phyllis Run, small cascades, boulders, scenic glen

Directions: From PA 949, turn onto the park road and follow for .2 mile to a small parking area on the left near picnic tables

The Phyllis Run Trail is a short loop with a cross connector trail that explores a scenic glen carved by its namesake. The glen features pines, hemlocks, spruce, and rhododendrons. From the parking area, proceed uphill above the run, with small cascades. Pass a juncture with the Radcliffe Trail to the left and continue to climb under spruce and hemlocks. Pass the connector trail to the right, which enables you to hike a shorter loop. Continue straight uphill along the stream. The trail turns right and crosses a bridge across a run. Begin a gradual descent across very rocky terrain.

Pass the connector trail and continue the descent. Notice how the terrain off to your right is extremely rocky, with boulders and outcrops that clutter the glen. Pass the Big Spring Trail to the left. The trail soon returns you to the park road.

49. Ridge and Clear Creek Trails

Duration: 2 to 3 hours

Distance: 2.7-mile loop

Difficulty: Moderate to difficult

Blazes: Korb Trail is blazed yellow; Clear Creek Trail white; Ridge Trail blue; and Phyllis Run Trail red

Terrain: Most descents and ascents are gradual, but the terrain along the Ridge Trail between Frazier and Clear Creek Trails is extremely steep

Elevation change: 350 feet

Trail conditions: Trails are generally well-blazed and established; some trails have old, faded blazes in various colors; parts of Ridge Trail is not blazed well.

Highlights: Clear Creek, Truby Run, cascades, hemlock and spruce forests, thick rhododendrons

Directions: From PA 949, turn onto the park road and follow for .2 mile to a small parking area on the left near picnic tables

From the parking area along the park road, descend along the Phyllis Run Trail and cross Clear Creek among picnic tables. Turn right onto the yellow-blazed Korb Trail as it closely follows Clear Creek downstream. Sections of this trail are not blazed well; simply follow

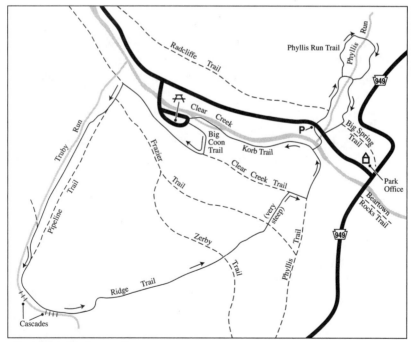

Hike 48: Phyllis Run Trail
Hike 49: Ridge and Clear Creek Trails

the established trail along the creek. Clear Creek is very scenic, with boulders, cascades, and deep pools. The trail climbs up the bank and follows an old grade. Cross a side channel without a bridge to an island in the creek. Hike across the small island and recross the side channel. This section can be very difficult in high water.

Turn left onto the Big Coon Trail at a picnic area and hike up the bank to another picnic area, where the trail turns left and proceeds upstream above the creek. It makes an increasingly steep ascent and reaches a juncture with the white-blazed Clear Creek Trail, where you turn right. Follow this trail for .4 mile as it traverses the side of the plateau. Pass boulders, including a low-lying rectangular one, and begin a gradual descent above the creek. The trail descends and turns right onto an unblazed pipeline swath; Clear Creek Trail continues straight.

Follow the wide, grassy swath gradually uphill until it forks in two. Both sections parallel each other closely and eventually rejoin, but the swath to the right is more scenic, as it is shaded with pines and provides views down into Truby Run's rhododendron jungle. A cross-country ski trail joins from the right and the two forks rejoin where Truby Run crosses the swath. Hike across the swath and bear left onto the blue-blazed Ridge Trail, which is hard to notice.

The trail crosses very rocky terrain above the run and then descends to the run, which features a variety of small falls and cascades in a scenic glen with thick rhododendrons. Proceed upstream along an old grade until the trail turns left and climbs away from the run. Hike through a hardwood forest and ascend steeply through dense mountain laurel that nearly crowds out the trail. When you reach the top of the trail, the forest becomes more open and the terrain is level. Here the trail is not well blazed in sections and has some blowdowns. After .6 mile, the trail reaches a juncture with Zerby Trail; continue straight on the Ridge Trail and begin a gradual descent. In another .2 mile, you pass the Frazier Trail. Continue straight on the Ridge Trail as it makes an extremely steep descent without switchbacks underneath a hemlock and spruce forest for .1 mile.

The Ridge Trail ends at the Clear Creek Trail. Turn right and follow this trail for a short distance. Turn left onto the Phyllis Run Trail, which descends under hemlocks and spruce to the Korb Trail, where you began your hike.

50. Hunters and Irish Rock Trails

Duration: 2 to 3 hours

Distance: 3-mile loop

Difficulty: Moderate to difficult

Blazes: All trails are blazed white except for the River Trail, which is yellow

Terrain: Level and rolling, with long ascents and descents

Elevation change: 350 feet

Trail conditions: Trails are generally well blazed and established

Highlights: Clarion River, Irish Rock, hemlock forests, mountain laurel, rhododendrons

Directions: From PA 949, follow the park road for 1.5 miles. In the cabin area, turn right toward the canoe launch. Traffic bears right at the beginning of the cabin loop. Follow the road to the end of the loop, where there is a parking area on the right.

With many natural features, this is one of the most scenic hikes in the state park. From the parking area, follow the white-blazed Hunters Trail as it ascends the plateau through thick mountain laurel and hardwoods. Sections of this climb are steep, without any switchbacks. The trail begins to level and passes large pine trees with mountain laurel. Upon reaching the top of the plateau, the hardwood forest becomes very open. The trail gradually moves closer to the rim of the plateau above the Clarion River, offering some views when the leaves are off the trees. After .5 mile, the trail turns right and begins a slight descent. Hike through thick laurel again and some pine trees. The trail reaches the rim of the plateau, where it turns left and follows the contour of the rim above Clear Creek.

Begin a gradual descent over rocky terrain into a hollow. Hike gradually out of the hollow and pass a juncture with the North Ridge Trail to your right; blazes are somewhat infrequent in this section. Continue straight for .2 mile, until you reach an unsigned juncture with a pipeline swath and park boundary. Follow the white-blazed Boundary Trail to the left. This trail crosses level terrain through a hardwood forest along the park boundary, which is also marked with white. The trail reaches the rim of the plateau and bends left as it gradually descends, until it suddenly turns right and follows level but very rocky terrain along the contour of the plateau among rhododendrons. The

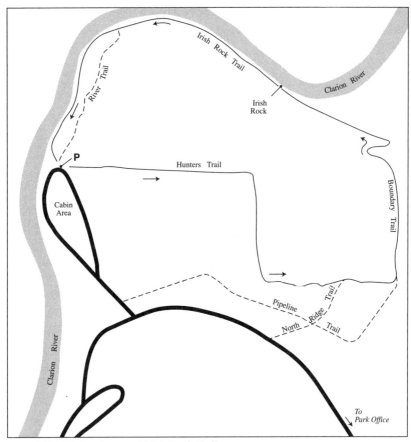

Hike 50: Hunters and Irish Rock Trails

trail returns to the park boundary, turns left, and goes down a steep bank to a grade and the Irish Rock Trail.

This beautiful trail gradually descends along the side of the plateau through a thick hemlock forest with rhododendrons. After .3 mile, you reach the river and Irish Rock, a large boulder used in the logging era by rafters to tie up and rest for the night. Notice the large eddy in front of the boulder and how the river's flow is constricted through a fast-moving channel. This is a great place to take a break and enjoy the beauty of the Clarion River.

The trail follows the river downstream, offering great views. Hardwoods become more prevalent, though hemlocks and rhododendrons are common along the river. The trail generally stays close to the river but occasionally meanders along the nearby lowlands. Near the end of the trail, continue along it to the right as it follows the ridge of a bank above the river and a side channel to the left through a tunnel of hemlocks and rhododendrons. Descend from the bank and bear right onto the yellow-blazed River Trail, which runs along the river downstream and offers similar scenery. Along one stretch, the trail is very close to the river. Climb steps up a bank and return to the parking area.

51. Tadler Run Trail

Duration: 2¹/₂ to 3¹/₂ hours

Distance: 4.8-mile loop

Difficulty: Moderate

Blazes: Tadler Run Trail is blazed green, Sawmill Trail white

Terrain: Most ascents and descents are gradual, but there is a steep section along Sawmill Trail

Elevation change: 400 feet

Trail conditions: Trails are generally well blazed and established; there are occasional benches along Tadler Run Trail

Highlights: Clarion River, hemlock forests, rhododendron tunnels, Truby Run, Clear Creek

Directions: From PA 949, follow the park road for .8 mile to a pipeline swath, picnic area, and parking area on the right

From the parking area, cross the bridge spanning Clear Creek and hike a short distance up the grassy pipeline swath. Turn right onto Clear Creek Trail and enter the woods. The trail crosses scenic Truby Run via a bridge and gradually ascends along an old grade above Clear Creek. Pass a juncture with Sawmill Trail to the left; you will return to this point. The forest changes from spruce and pines to hardwoods as the trail passes a juncture with the Ox Shoe Trail to the right. Continue along the grade until it ends at a paved road in the campground. Follow the road to the left, passing campsites and large boulders. The road descends to the end of the campground loop; bear left onto a spur road and hike past more campsites. At the end of the road, the green-blazed Tadler Run Trail begins to the left.

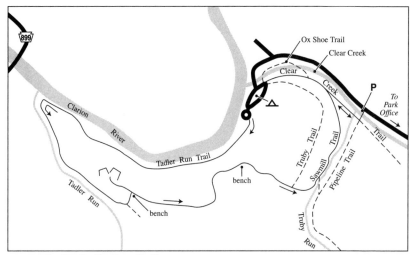

Hike 51: Tadler Run Trail

Follow the trail as it gradually ascends an old forest road along the contour of the plateau. The trail stays about 100 feet above the river. Although the trail is established, parts of the grade are brushy. Hemlocks are common along the river, while hardwoods dominate the higher slopes. The trail curves through a side glen and maintains its elevation as it passes through a thick hemlock forest. The river is out of view as the trail descends to the river valley, with large pine trees and hemlocks. The trail bears left and the river gradually comes into view. The PA 899 bridge is just downstream.

Begin a gradual ascent through thick hemlocks as the trail makes a sharp left and follows another grade above Tadler Run. For the next .6 mile, the trail gradually ascends this stream valley with only an occasional glimpse of the run, which flows far below through a rhododendron jungle. A highlight of this trail is the walls of rhododendrons growing on both sides of the trail. Although Tadler Run is just off to your right and can be heard, you never see it because of the thick rhododendrons and hemlocks. As the trail reaches the plateau, the hemlocks and rhododendrons diminish and hardwoods dominate the forest.

Keep a close eye for the trail, which turns left where an obvious grade continues straight. Reach a bench and a .2-mile side trail, blazed with a green "L," that goes to a rock outcrop covered with rhododendrons. Although the park map says there is a view here the trees in front of the outcrop are too high, so any views are limited to when the leaves are off the trees.

The trail continues along the top of the plateau, passing groves of spruce and pines and a few open meadows along a private-property line. Follow the trail as it curves to the left and returns to the steep edge of the plateau at another bench. Again, the park map indicates a view, but there isn't one. The trail crosses the top of the plateau and begins a gradual descent among outcrops and small boulders, until it reaches a juncture with Truby and Sawmill Trails and another bench.

Follow the Sawmill Trail as it descends very steeply to Truby Run. This scenic run has many cascades under a cloak of hemlocks, spruce, and rhododendrons. Pass a cross-country ski trail to the right and follow the run closely downstream. The trail then climbs away from the run but soon returns at a bend with many cascades. Follow a grade above the run and proceed gradually downstream away from the run. The trail curves to the left and begins a long descent to Clear Creek Trail, which is just below, but it is some distance before the two trails meet. Turn right and retrace your steps to the parking area.

52. Pine Run Trail

Duration: 1 hour

Distance: .7 mile (one-way)

Difficulty: Moderate

Blazes: Faded orange

Terrain: Long, gradual descent and ascent

Elevation change: 300 feet

Trail conditions: Trail is fairly well blazed and follows an established grade

Highlights: Pine Run, Clarion River, pine and hemlock forest, unusual root formations

Directions: From the state park, proceed 1.8 miles north on PA 949 to a small bridge across Pine Run. There is very limited space along the road to park.

This short, forgotten trail explores a scenic glen carved by Pine Run and features a deep pine and hemlock forest with rock outcrops and boulders. Rhododendrons are prevalent along the stream on the lower half of the hike. The real highlight, however, is the surprising number of trees with incredible root formations. Webs of roots encase

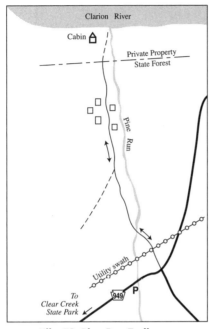

Hike 52: Pine Run Trail

boulders; one tree actually looks as though it is stepping off a boulder. Dozens of other trees are supported by their roots, as if they are on stilts. This happens when a tree grows out of the rotting stump of another, and the roots are exposed as the stump decomposes. Root formations always seem to fascinate hikers, especially children. This is a great place to take some interesting pictures.

From PA 949, follow an old grade with occasional faded orange blazes. Cross a utility line swath and descend to a footbridge across the run. Follow the grade down the glen and pass through an area with a lot of root formations. Rhododendrons become more common, as do rock outcrops and boulders. The grade steepens and is rocky in places. Pine Run can be heard off to your right but is usually out of sight.

The blazed trail ends at a trail sign and the state forest boundary, marked in white. The grade continues through thick rhododendrons to the Clarion River. A large cabin is off to your left. There weren't any No Trespassing signs when I hiked here, but I don't know whether hiking is permitted to the river. Retrace your steps to PA 949.

🥾 53. Clear Creek Trail

Duration: 2½ to 3 hours

Distance: 3.8-mile loop

Difficulty: Moderate

Blazes: Orange

Terrain: Gradual ascents and descents

Elevation change: 300 feet

Trail conditions: Trails are generally well blazed and established, with bridges across most stream crossings

Highlights: Clear Creek, Little Clear Creek, rhododendron tunnels, interpretive signs

Directions: The parking area is located on the left along PA 949, at Picnic Shelter 5, just before the entrance to the state park

This loop offers a lot of isolation and scenery; do not confuse it with Clear Creek Trail in the state park. From the parking area, follow PA 949 past the juncture with Corbett Road and the park office for .2 mile. The loop begins on the right just past the forestry buildings, where there is a trail sign. Descend to Little Clear Creek and cross a bridge.

The trail gradually ascends the valley of this small stream along an old forest grade, passing small cascades, hemlocks, spruce, and rhododendrons. Cross the run four times on bridges and pass a half-mile-long side trail to the left that ascends to a parking area along PA 949. This side trail is .8 mile from the beginning of the Clear Creek Trail. Cross the run a final time and hike through a hardwood forest; to your left, Little Clear Creek flows through a ravine covered in rhododendrons. Follow the run almost to its source, until you reach the plateau in a forestry demonstration area with several interpretive signs. Cross Little Clear Creek Road, which is 1.6 miles from the start of the trail.

The trail becomes less established as it cuts through spruce and laurel along a meadow to the right. Begin a slight descent through an open hardwood forest. After .4 mile from the road, you reach a pipeline swath and the Silvis Trail to the left. The Clear Creek Trail bears right and descends to the headwaters of a stream. As you descend, you pass seep springs and rhododendrons become increasingly common, nearly crowding out the trail. A stream can be heard babbling off to the right. The terrain is rocky and slippery. Tunnel through a thick rhododendron jungle and reach a bridge across Clear Creek. The trail intersects an unmarked trail to the left and bears right through a thick, impressive tunnel

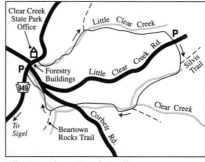

Hike 53: Clear Creek Trail

of rhododendrons. The trail soon crosses Clear Creek again and follows an old grade above the creek through a hardwood forest with mountain laurel. Thick rhododendrons encompass Clear Creek to the left. Pass through a red pine grove and cross Corbett Road.

Continue along the trail to another bridge across Clear Creek and bear right onto Beartown Rocks Trail. Follow the creek closely through thick spruce and red pines. Pass the remains of a logging dam and cross the creek. The trail goes through a meadow, the site of an old oil well, and enters a spruce grove. Cross another bridge and continue to hike through a thick spruce grove before entering the hardwood forest. The trail returns to the creek, crossing a small side stream, and passes underneath spruce and red pines along scenic Clear Creek. It then goes back to PA 949 and the parking area.

 ## 54. Beartown Rocks Trail

Duration: 2 to 3 hours

Distance: 1.8 miles (one-way)

Difficulty: Moderate

Blazes: Orange

Terrain: Level, with gradual ascents and descents

Elevation change: 540 feet

Trail conditions: Trail is well established and blazed

Highlights: Beartown Rocks, vista, Clear Creek, Trap Run, rhododendrons, pines, spruce, interpretive signs

Directions: The parking area is located on the left along PA 949, at Picnic Shelter 5 just before the entrance to the state park

This is probably the most popular trail in Clear Creek. It ascends a valley to Beartown Rocks, a large rock city offering an expansive view to the north. You can lengthen your hike by returning via the Trap Run Loop Trail.

From the parking area, cross PA 949 and follow the trail along Clear Creek through a thick grove of spruce and red pines. Along the trail are interpretive signs about the logging era. Cross a bridge across a side stream and enter a hardwood forest. The trail turns left and enters a thick spruce grove before crossing Clear Creek via a bridge. Continue through a spruce grove and pass through a large meadow, once the site of an oil well. The trail crosses another bridge over Clear Creek and passes along the stream under spruce and pines. Hike over the remains of an old logging dam.

Reach a juncture with the Clear Creek Trail to the left. The Beartown Rocks Trail bears right and follows an old forest road lined with thick rhododendrons. Pass Trap Run Loop Trail to the right, and soon thereafter, cross Trap Run at a gas well. Continue along the old forest road through a thick understory of rhododendrons in a hardwood forest.

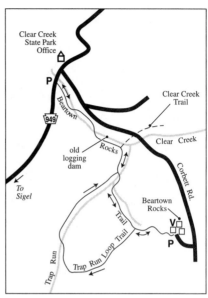

Hike 54: Beartown Rocks Trail

Cross a small side stream and bear left as the trail makes a steeper ascent up the valley. As you climb, the rhododendrons recede and the hardwood forest becomes more open. Reach the plateau and cross level terrain before passing through a ravine. Continue along level terrain and pass another juncture with the Trap Run Loop Trail. The Beartown Rocks Trail continues straight and enters an open area, where it turns right onto a grassy forest road. Follow this road for a short distance, then turn left onto the trail as it ascends to a parking area. The rocks are just to the left, and steps lead to a beautiful vista overlooking the plateau to the north. If you look closely, you can tell where the Clarion River flows. The rock city is a fascinating place to explore, with massive boulders.

Return the way you came. If you'd like to extend your hike, turn left onto the first juncture with the Trap Run Loop Trail (which was the second juncture on your hike up to the rocks). This trail is well blazed but not as well established or maintained. It is level but makes a gradual descent into the stream valley, with pines and rhododendrons. Descend along the stream, then cross it as the trail follows an old grade. The trail is above the stream, which flows through a rhododendron jungle and returns to the Beartown Rocks Trail. This route will add about an hour to your hike.

State Game Lands 74

State Game Lands (SGL) 74 covers almost 7,000 acres and envelops much of Mill Creek, a tributary of the Clarion River. In the eastern section is the Baker Trail as it follows Mill Creek for about 2.5 miles. In the western section, the creek is larger and has carved a rugged gorge. An old forest road winds along the gorge on the southern side of the creek, making for an enjoyable hike.

Contact information: Pennsylvania Game Commission Northwest Region, PO Box 31, Franklin, PA 16323; phone: 814-432-3188; website: www.pgc. state.pa.us

🚶🚶 55. Baker Trail

Duration: 2¹/₂ to 4 hours

Distance: 2.5 miles (one-way)

Difficulty: Easy

Blazes: Yellow

Terrain: Rolling and level

Elevation change: 100 feet

Trail conditions: Trail is fairly well blazed and established

Highlights: Mill Creek, pine forest, meadows

Directions: From the small village of Fisher, follow Hudson Road (SR 1003) south for 1.2 miles. Turn left onto Old State Road and follow for 1.4 miles to a new concrete bridge across Mill Creek. You can park on the left before crossing the bridge, where the hike begins. A large lot is also across the bridge on the right. From I-80, take Exit 70 and follow US 322 east for .3 mile. Take the first left onto Potter Road and follow for .6 mile. Turn right onto Asbury Road and follow for 4.5 miles to the concrete bridge and parking areas.

The Baker Trail is a 141-mile-long backpacking trail that stretches from Freeport to the Allegheny National Forest. Much of it follows roads and utility-line rights-of-way. As a result, the trail has been designated an endangered hiking trail by the Keystone Trails Association. If you'd like to help maintain and protect this popular trail, contact the Harmony Trails Council, PO Box 243, Ingomar, PA 18127, or visit www.harmonytrails.com or www.rachelcarsontrail.com. This hike follows a 2.5-mile segment of the Baker Trail along Mill Creek.

From the parking area, hike upstream on the north side of Mill Creek a few yards. Cross McKanna Run and notice the Baker Trail, blazed yellow. To the left, the trail climbs up the glen of McKanna Run. Follow the trail straight as it heads upstream along Mill Creek, with boulders, pools, and babbling rapids. This stretch of trail is often wet, and hemlocks are common. Begin a gradual climb along the grade, which is somewhat overgrown, but the trail can still be followed. Mill Creek is out of sight as it flows in a deep glen to your right. After .6 mile from the parking area, bear right onto a gated dirt road. Follow this road for .5 mile underneath hemlocks and pines; Mill Creek is out of sight but can be heard.

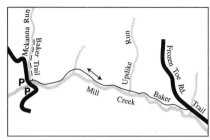

Hike 55: Baker Trail

The trail then bears right onto a grassy grade as the dirt road ascends to the left. This is a scenic stretch as the trail follows the creek closely, with hemlocks, pools, and small boulders. The trail rejoins another gated road and soon passes through a large meadow with views of Mill Creek. Cross the meadow and Updike Run. The trail begins to meander through a pine forest along an old grade. Mill Creek flows off to your left. After .3 mile from the meadow, the trail passes near the creek for the last time. It moves away from the creek through a deep, mysterious pine forest for an additional .6 mile before ending at Frozen Toe Road. Retrace your steps back to your car.

 56. Mill Creek Gorge

Duration: 2½ to 4 hours

Distance: 2.7 miles (one-way)

Difficulty: Easy to moderate

Blazes: None

Terrain: Rolling and level, with long ascents and descents

Elevation change: 250 feet

Trail conditions: Trail is well established, since it follows an obvious gated forest road, but it is not blazed

Highlights: Mill Creek Gorge, hemlocks, thick rhododendrons, cascades along Whites Creek

Directions: From I-80, take Exit 70 and proceed west on US 322 for 3.1 miles. Turn right onto SR 1001 and follow for almost 3 miles as it descends to Mill Creek. A large pull-off area is on the right before the road crosses the creek. The beginning of the hike is the across the road, off to the left. To reach the Millcreek Road trailhead from I-80, take US 322 west for 4.4 miles to Strattanville. Turn right onto SR 1011 and follow for .2 mile; bear left onto Millcreek Road and follow for 1.8 miles to a small parking area on the right. Do not block the gate.

This hike follows a gated forest road as it climbs along the Mill Creek Gorge. Here Mill Creek has carved a surprisingly rugged 400-foot-deep gorge into the plateau as it descends to the Clarion River. Hemlocks and rhododendrons are prevalent along this trail, especially the eastern half. As a result, this is an ideal trail to hike in late June or early July, when the rhododendrons bloom. For much of this hike, Mill Creek is out of sight,

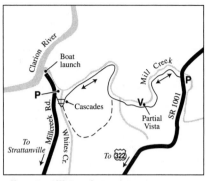

Hike 56: Mill Creek Gorge

but it is not out of sound, as its rapids are clearly heard. Unlike the segment of Mill Creek you encounter on the Baker Trail hike, here it has grown into a large stream with Class II rapids that attract kayakers. Despite the beauty and wilderness of the gorge, which is completely untouched by development, Mill Creek is stained orange from acid mine drainage.

From the parking area, cross SR 1001 and hike around the gate. Follow the grade across level terrain for .5 mile, with hemlocks and thick jungles of rhododendrons. You are offered only a brief view of Mill Creek. Begin a gradual climb under thick hemlocks and occasional rhododendrons. The climb continues until you are about 200 feet above Mill Creek; the terrain to the right is extremely steep and there are partial views of the gorge, especially when the leaves are off the trees. Hardwoods dominate the forest, with a thick understory of rhododendrons. Begin a gradual descent and reenter a hemlock forest. The grade crosses over a small, cascading stream before beginning a gradual ascent as the trail enters a hardwood forest 1.6 miles from the parking area.

The trail returns to the level of the creek with some views of the rapids. Begin another gradual ascent away from the creek underneath hemlocks. Avoid a forest road to the left and cross over Whites Creek, with many cascades and small falls. To the right, Whites Creek tumbles down a steep glen cloaked in hemlocks, with several small waterfalls. Hike the grade an additional .1 mile across level terrain to gravel Millcreek Road. Return the way you came.

Tionesta Lake

Tionesta Lake is formed by a 154-foot-high dam that was completed in 1940. The lake is 6.3 miles long, with 12 miles of shoreline, and covers 480 acres at summer pool. Camping is a popular activity at Tionesta Lake, with two campgrounds beneath the dam along Tionesta Creek and several wilderness boat-in campsites along the shoreline. Tionesta Creek and Lake are surrounded by steep hillsides that add to the beauty of the site. There are five short trails near the dam that offer relatively easy hikes with views of the lake.

Contact information: Tionesta Lake, PO Box 539, Tionesta, PA 16353-9801; phone: 814-755-3512; website: www.lrp.usace.army.mil/rec/lakes/tionesta.htm

57. Summit, Plantation, and Information Center Loop Trails

Duration: 1 to 2 hours

Distance: Summit Trail is a .8-mile loop; Plantation Trail is a .4-mile linear trail; Information Center Loop Trail is a .25-mile loop

Difficulty: Easy to moderate

Blazes: None

Terrain: Level and rolling, with gradual inclines and declines

Elevation change: 100 feet

Trail conditions: Trails are generally well established, with signs at junctures. The Information Center Loop Trail is paved.

Highlights: Partial views of Tionesta Lake, pine and spruce plantations, wetlands.

Directions: From Tionesta, follow PA 36 south for 1.3 miles. Turn left to Tionesta Lake and cross the top of the dam to a traffic circle. To reach the Information Center Loop Trail, make the first right. For the other trails, make the second right and park in the parking area across from the ranger office.

Begin by hiking the Summit Trail, the longest and most difficult of all the trails. Cross an access road (keep this road in your mind for later in the hike) and follow several gradual switchbacks along old grades through a hardwood forest before climbing through a pine plantation. Soon thereafter, you reach a bench with a partial wintertime view over Tionesta Lake. Descend along more switchbacks, with benches, and hike along a series of concrete posts. To the right is the dam's emergency spillway. The trail turns left and climbs gradually to a grove of pine trees. Pick up another grade and descend slightly, passing a vista to the west.

Turn right and descend the bank along the Plantation Trail. Follow boardwalks between two small ponds. The trail meanders through a hardwood forest and meadows before entering a large pine plantation. Turn right in the plantation and hike down a column of trees until you reach an electric-line swath. The Plantation Trail continues straight to a road and a trail that descends to the dam and campground. To make a loop, hike the electric-line swath to the left for .14 mile between spruce and pine plantations.

When you reach the access road mentioned previously, turn left as it tunnels through pines and spruce. The road enters an opening and bears right, rejoining with the Summit Trail and returning to the parking area.

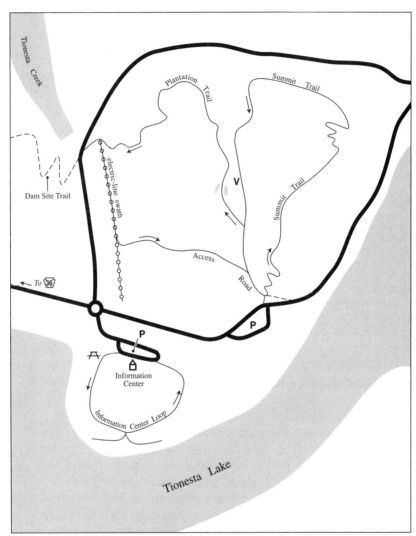

Hike 57: Summit, Plantation, and Information Center Loop Trails

The Information Center Loop Trail is a great trail for small children. This paved trail begins and ends at the Information Center and encircles a large field. From the center, begin the loop to the right, or counterclockwise. The trail descends slightly past picnic tables to the edge of a steep bank above the reservoir, where you reach benches and a partial view of the lake; two trails descend to the lake. The trail returns to the center across a field.

Cornplanter
State Forest

At 1,354 acres, Cornplanter is one of the smallest state forests in Pennsylvania. The forest was named after Chief Cornplanter of the Seneca tribe. He helped maintain peace between the new American government and the Iroquois between 1784 and 1812. Chief Cornplanter remains a well-known historical figure in the region to this day.

Cornplanter State Forest is composed of two tracts. The larger, by far, is located near Tionesta and features more than 8 miles of trails. Backcountry camping is permitted along these trails. The gem of the state forest is the beautiful old-growth forest of the Anders Run Natural Area, located a few miles from Youngsville.

Contact information: Cornplanter State Forest, 323 North State Street, North Warren, PA 16365; phone: 814-723-0262; website: www.dcnr.state. pa.us/forestry/stateforests/cornplanter.aspx

58. Lashure and Hunter Run Trails

Duration: 1 to 2 hours

Distance: 2.4-mile loop

Difficulty: Easy to moderate

Blazes: Lashure Trail has blue blazes, Hunter Run Trail orange

Terrain: Level and rolling, with gradual ascents and descents

Elevation change: 100 feet

Trail conditions: Trails are well established and blazed

Highlights: Interpretive trail, pine plantations, forest history

Directions: From Tionesta, follow PA 36 north for 2.5 miles and turn right onto Neiltown Road. Drive for 1.1 miles to the forestry office, trailhead, and parking on the left.

The Hunter Run tract constitutes most of the Cornplanter State Forest and is home to more than 8 miles of hiking loops and connector trails. Because of windstorm damage, the McCaferty Run and Marfink Trails were closed when I visited the state forest. The forest is typical of the region, with expansive open hardwoods and a few hemlocks and pines.

From the parking area, follow the road to the left past the forestry office and begin to hike the blue-blazed Lashure Trail, an interpretive trail. Pass through a pine plantation and enter a hardwood forest as the trail gently ascends. Cross a bridge over a small stream and another over a wet area. An orange-blazed trail joins from the right. Stay on the Lashure Trail as it continues its moderate ascent. At the height of the land, the trail turns left and begins a mild descent along a private-property line to the right.

Reach a juncture where the Lashure Trail descends to the left; follow orange-blazed Trail 3 straight along rolling terrain. Notice the ground pine on the forest floor. Begin a steeper descent and pass a juncture with Trail 4 to the left. Bear right as the trail returns to a forest road; the parking area is to the left. Take an immediate right onto an orange-blazed trail as it descends to Neiltown Road. Cross the road and continue the descent to a bridge over Hunter Run. Begin a mild ascent and cross another bridge over a wet area. Turn left and follow

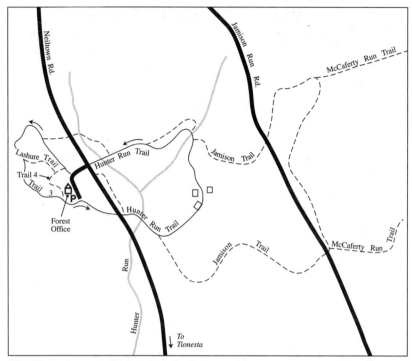

Hike 58: Lashure and Hunter Run Trails

Hunter Run at a juncture with the blue-blazed Jamison Trail to the right. Follow the contour along the plateau and pass a few boulders. Begin a mild descent to the stream valley and cross a bridge over a wet area.

The Jamison Trail rejoins from the right; cross another bridge over a small stream. Follow Hunter Run Trail to the left as the Jamison Trail leaves to the right. Ascend and follow the contour of the plateau. Cross another bridge over a seasonal stream. The Jamison Trail rejoins from the right; begin a long, gradual descent. Before reaching the stream, the Hunter Trail leaves to the right; follow the blue-blazed Jamison Trail and cross the bridge over Hunter Run. Cross Neiltown Road and hike the road past the forestry office and back to the parking area.

59. Anders Run Natural Area

Duration: 2 to 3 hours

Distance: 2-mile loop

Difficulty: Easy to moderate

Blazes: Main trail loop is blazed yellow; cross connector red

Terrain: Rolling terrain, with short, steep climbs. The yellow trail explores the top of the banks above the run.

Elevation change: 150 feet

Trail conditions: Trail is well blazed and established. Along the southern side of the loop is eroded narrow sidehill. Most stream crossings have bridges, and there are trail signs and benches.

Highlights: Anders Run, Stone House, trout fishing, old-growth forest with white pines and hemlock, wildflowers

Directions: From the intersection of US 6 and US 62, located 6 miles west of Warren, proceed south on US 62 for .4 mile. Make the next right onto SR 3022 and follow for .8 mile. Turn left onto Dunns Eddy River Road and follow for 1 mile to the trailhead and parking area on the left.

Anders Run is the only natural area in the Cornplanter State Forest and offers an impressive old-growth white pine and hemlock forest in a scenic stream valley. The natural area protects one of the most beautiful forests in northwestern Pennsylvania.

From the parking area, look down the road a short distance and notice a trail sign; this marks the end of your hike. Begin by descending the yellow-blazed trail along an old forest grade. You soon enter a white pine forest with several large specimens. Descend and bear right along the trail underneath the massive pines. Upon reaching Dunns Eddy River Road, follow the trail to the left and descend along the road. Once you reach the bottom of the valley, notice the Stone House off to your left. This home was built in 1841 by a local farmer; one of the walls appears to be buckling.

Leave the road and follow the trail to your right. You soon enter an ancient forest of white pines and hemlocks. Cross a bridge over a seasonal side stream and continue to hike up the valley floor. Off to your left is Anders Run, a pristine stream that has pools small cascades and is choked with logs and woody debris—a perfect combination for brook trout. Upon reaching the second bridge that crosses Anders Run, the red-blazed cross connector trail leaves to the right. This trail is less than .25 mile long and connects with the main loop on the northern side. It passes through the old-growth forest, crosses a seasonal side stream, and ascends to Sulfer Spring Road. It crosses the

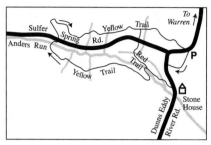

Hike 59: Anders Run Natural Area

road and soon rejoins with the yellow loop trail. You can take the red-blazed trail to significantly shorten your hike.

Otherwise, cross the bridge along the yellow trail and head downstream along the run, passing a cascade and deep pool. The trail swings right and proceeds uphill above the exposed roots of a fallen tree. When it reaches the edge of the bank above the run, the trail becomes rolling, but the sidehill is narrow and eroded. For the next .7 mile, the trail stays on the bank above the run, offering great views into the valley. The trees seem even more impressive when you look at them from the top of the bank. Notice the striking difference between the forest that lies within the natural area and that on the private land off to your left. The forest in the natural area is verdant, impressive, and diverse, whereas the forest on the private land is filled with brush and immature hardwoods.

Pass through the small ravines of springs and begin to descend back to Anders Run. The trail makes a sharp right and the descent steepens. The trail crosses the run; when I hiked here last, there wasn't a bridge. Cross Sulfer Spring Road and begin to hike the northern half of the loop, which contains large white pines but is dominated by hardwoods.

The trail gradually climbs to an old forest road. Leave the road after crossing a small stream. The terrain is rolling and not as precipitous as on the southern half of the trail. Cross two more seasonal side streams and hike underneath pine trees. Pass some rock outcrops and boulders, including one with a hemlock growing out of it. The red-blazed cross connector trail joins from the right. Cross another seasonal stream and climb a hill. Descend to Dunns Eddy River Road and turn left to the parking area and your car.

State Game
Lands 282

State Game Lands (SGL) 282 covers about 500 acres along Conewango Creek and the New York border. This area has diverse habitats—wetlands, woodlands, meadows, and small ponds—that are home to a variety of plants and animals.

Contact information: Pennsylvania Game Commission Northwest Region, PO Box 31, Franklin, PA 16323; phone: 814-432-3188; website: www.pgc. state.pa.us.

🚶🚶 60. Akeley Swamp

Duration: 1 hour

Distance: 1.1 mile (one-way)

Difficulty: Easy

Blazes: None

Terrain: Level

Elevation change: 5 feet

Trail conditions: Trail follows an old railroad grade that is clearly established

Highlights: Akeley Swamp, Conewango Creek, swamps, wetlands, wildlife

Directions: From the intersection of US 62 north and Business Route 6 in downtown Warren, proceed north on US 62 for 8.6 miles. Turn right onto Ackeley/Old US 62. Bear left onto SR 1015 and follow for 1.6 miles. Turn left onto Martin Road (T625) and follow for .7 mile to a parking area.

A friend of mine, Steve Davis, is an avid hunter and told me about Akeley Swamp after scouting the area for deer. He reported a surprising amount of wildlife, especially amphibians and turtles. Naturally, I decided to check out the area, a reconstituted wetland, to see if I could include it in this guide. If you enjoy wildlife- or bird-watching, this is an ideal trail. It offers some of the best wildlife-watching in the ANF region, because it overlooks an extensive area of wetlands several hundred acres in size. Akeley Swamp is known as an important birding area, and is home to numerous waterfowl, songbirds, and raptors. Don't forget to bring your binoculars.

From the parking area, turn right onto an old railroad grade that is now a gated road. This grade is straight and level, and you will need to return the way you came. After .2 mile, cross a bridge. After another .1 mile, extensive wetlands come into view on your right and a young deciduous forest on your left. For the next .6 mile, the grade borders the wetlands and offers a great panorama to observe wildlife. Gentle hills rise in the distance. On the far side of the wetlands are towering white pine trees. Off to your right, notice the obvious difference between the wetlands and the mature deciduous forest interspersed with hemlocks. The grade crosses a second short bridge .4 mile from the parking area. Soon thereafter, the Conewango Creek comes into view to your left. Notice an unblazed trail that descends from the grade to the left and

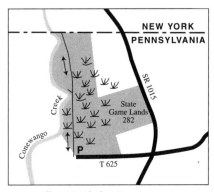

Hike 60: Akeley Swamp

offers a nice view of the creek as it meanders through the woodlands. The Conewango is a large creek and makes for a great canoe trip. Return to the grade.

At .7 mile from the parking area, cross another bridge, with a dam-like structure that holds water for the wetlands. After this last bridge, the grade continues for .4 mile to a gate and the New York border. This remaining part of the grade is somewhat grassy and overgrown. Thick brush also grows along this section, so there are no views of the wetlands. Retrace your steps to the parking area.

Backpacking Trails

The ANF is a popular backpacking destination, particularly because of the rising popularity of the North Country Trail. Tracy Ridge, Minister Creek, Tanbark, Morrison, and Hickory Creek Trails have long attracted backpackers. The forest contains numerous backpacking opportunities, with trails that vary in length, difficulty, and scenery.

61. North Country National Scenic Trail

The North Country National Scenic Trail (NCT) is envisioned to ultimately stretch 4,600 miles from North Dakota to New York. Once completed, it will be the longest trail in the country. It is now the longest trail in the Allegheny National Forest and northwest Pennsylvania. The NCT serves as a backbone to the forest's trail system; many of the forest's other trails are connected to it.

As one of Pennsylvania's three national scenic trails, the NCT continues to grow in popularity. The trail features scenic streams, the Allegheny Reservoir, old-growth forests, boulders and outcrops, and beautiful camping. It often follows and crosses old or established forest roads and old grades. Pipelines, oil and gas wells, and pumps are also found along the trail corridor.

The NCT from New York to Gravel Lick Road is the longest established section of the trail in Pennsylvania. Other sections have been constructed in Moraine and McConnell's Mill State Parks. Moraine features a large lake and a shelter. McConnell's Mill is a place of great natural beauty, in a rugged gorge with waterfalls, whitewater, and cliffs.

The ANF publishes a free brochure with a map and brief description of the trail. Maps of the trail can also be purchased from the North Country Trail Association.

The description below follows the trail from the New York border to Gravel Lick Road near Cook Forest State Park and is divided into four sections.

Contact information: North Country Trail Association, 229 East Main Street, Lowell, MI 49331; phone: 1-888-454-6282; e-mail: HQ@northcountry trail.org; websites: www.northcountrytrail.org/explore/ex_pa/pa.htm and www.dcnr.state.pa.us/forestry/hiking/north.htm. Allegheny National Forest, PO Box 847, Warren, PA 16365; phone: 814-723-5150; websites: www.fs. fed.us/r9/forests/allegheny and www.allegheny-online.com/hikingtrails.html.

Section I:
New York Border to Red Bridge

Duration: 2 to 3 days

Distance: 29.2 miles

Difficulty: Moderate to difficult

Blazes: Blue

Water: Generally plentiful; trail crosses many streams and is often in close proximity to the Allegheny Reservoir

Vegetation: Open hardwoods with ferns most common; scenic hemlock and pine forests generally on north-facing slopes or along streams; occasional pine plantations

Terrain: Descents and ascents are gradual, with the most difficult terrain between Handsome Lake Campground and Nelse Run

Elevation change: 600 feet

Trail conditions: Well blazed and established; some sidehill along the Allegheny Reservoir is worn out; often follows and crosses old forest roads and grades; some sections brushy and boggy

Highlights: Allegheny Reservoir, Allegheny National Recreation Area, scenic streams, good campsites, rock outcrops, hemlock forests

Directions:

Schoolhouse Hollow (PA 346): Trailhead and small parking area are located along PA 346 on the right, .9 mile west of the juncture with PA 321.

PA 59: Trailhead is located along PA 59, almost 25 miles west of Smethport and 15.5 miles east of the PA 59 juncture with US 6, near Warren. Turn onto the dirt forest road on the south side of PA 59 to reach the parking area.

PA 321: From the juncture of PA 59 and PA 321, at the Bradford Ranger Station, take PA 321 south 4.6 miles to a small parking area. From Kane, take PA 321 14 miles north.

Red Bridge: From the juncture of PA 59 and PA 321, at the Bradford Ranger Station, take PA 321 south 9.5 miles to a parking area on the right before the bridge. From Kane, take PA 321 9 miles north.

With great views across the Allegheny Reservoir, scenic streams, and beautiful campsites, this section is probably the most popular in the forest. It also presents fewer road crossings and offers a greater sense of wilderness.

From the New York border, the trail descends steeply for 300 feet over .3 mile into Schoolhouse Run's valley. Reach the small run and proceed downstream. At one point, the trail crosses and follows the streambed. Pick up an old grade and continue a moderate descent; the run flows off to your left and is out of sight. Reach a small parking area along PA 346; the trail turns left and follows this road.

Cross the road bridge over Willow Creek and descend to a level area. The trail follows an old grade to the left, but then curves to the right and begins a gradual ascent along the contour of the plateau. Cross over several small seasonal streams. After 1.5 miles, the trail ascends and passes through a saddle between two ridges. The NCT maintains its elevation along the contour of the plateau before descending slightly to small Williams Brook. Cross the seasonal brook and continue along level terrain for .5 mile. The trail bends to the left and descends more steeply for .4 mile. It then switchbacks to the right and descends to North Branch at its confluence with Tracy Run and the Allegheny Reservoir. This is a beautiful inlet with excellent campsites along the streams.

Cross the streams and follow the trail above the inlet. The Tracy Ridge Trail joins from the left. Follow narrow sidehill along a steep bank above the reservoir and reach a point where the trail makes a sharp left, with nice views over the reservoir. Continue to follow narrow sidehill and begin a gradual ascent away from the reservoir. After a mile, cross a small seasonal stream and continue the gradual ascent; the reservoir is out of view when leaves are on the trees. Enter the shallow glen of Whiskey Run; the trail crosses the small run and maintains its elevation along the contour of the plateau before descending back to the reservoir and the inlet of Johnnycake Run, with scenic campsites on the north side of the inlet. The Johnnycake Trail joins from the left, and the NCT crosses the run of that name.

The NCT now bears right and gradually ascends above the inlet before making a short, steep ascent. The trail turns left and meets an old forest road, on which it bears left. Follow this old road as it gradually ascends, bears left, and descends into a hemlock-shaded glen with a small stream. A side trail to the right descends to the scenic Handsome Lake campground along the reservoir. Handsome Lake is a boat- or hike-in campground, with picnic tables, water, pit toilets, and beautiful views over the reservoir. To use this campground, you must self-register and pay a fee.

From here, the NCT climbs up the scenic glen, turns right, and crosses the small stream. Begin a steeper 250-foot climb over .3 mile to the top of the ridge. At the top, the gray-blazed Tracy Ridge Hiking Trail System proceeds straight and descends to Hopewell Campground,

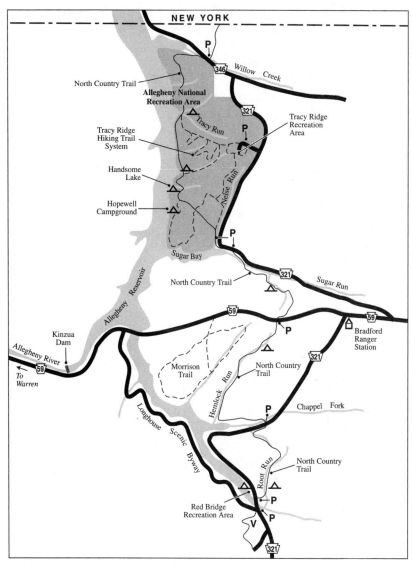

Section I: New York Border to Red Bridge

while the NCT turns left and follows the top of the ridge along level
and rolling terrain. At one point, the terrain drops steeply from both
sides of the trail. The trail reaches the edge of the plateau and begins a
long, 1.5-mile descent over 500 feet as it follows an old grade into a
beautiful glen of a tributary to Nelse Run. Thick hemlocks cover this

glen. Reach the bottom and cross the beautiful Nelse Run over a bridge; a side trail to the left climbs to a small parking area along PA 321. For the next .7 mile, the trail is level as it follows sidehill below PA 321 and above the reservoir.

Bear right onto PA 321 and follow for .2 mile before the trail turns from the road and descends to another. Cross a bridge over Sugar Run and follow the run upstream for a short distance across boggy terrain. Turn right onto an old forest road and ascend 100 feet above Sugar Run, then turn left and follow another old grade along the level contour of the plateau for .9 mile. The NCT descends slightly and enters the scenic wooded valley of Hammond Run. Gradually ascend up the valley as the trail closely follows the run. Pass a side stream to the right, where there are nice campsites. After .9 mile, cross the run and begin to climb away from it; the trail turns left and gradually ascends before turning right to reach the top of the plateau. For the next mile, gradually ascend along the top of the plateau. Bear right onto a road and hike to PA 59.

Cross PA 59 and follow a dirt forest road past a small parking area. Turn right and follow level terrain across fern meadows, with a slight descent to the headwaters of Hemlock Run. The NCT begins a long, 600-foot descent over 3 miles as it follows the scenic Hemlock Run down its valley, at times following old grades. Small potential campsites can be found along Hemlock Run. As the trail nears the reservoir, it turns left and is level for .5 mile before dropping down to Chappel Fork. Cross Briggs Run and ascend 100 feet up the side of the plateau, then follow the level contour for .5 mile. Cross Coon Run and turn right as the trail descends and crosses Chappel Fork. Climb to PA 321, where there is a small parking area.

Cross PA 321 and follow a forest road to the right for .3 mile above the state highway. The NCT bears left and climbs more steeply before entering the glen of a small stream. Ascend 500 feet over a mile to the top of the plateau. Begin a slight descent, cross a forest road, and descend more steeply to Root Run. Cross the run and follow it downstream; after 1.5 miles, turn left and recross the run. Potential campsites along the run can be found in this area. Climb and descend along the flank of the plateau before reaching a forest road and PA 321. The entrance to Red Bridge Recreation Area is to the right, where there are campsites, picnic tables, water, and showers for a fee. Across PA 321 is a pull-off parking area. The NCT turns left and follows PA 321 across the reservoir.

Section II:
Red Bridge to Henrys Mills

Duration: 1½ to 2½ days

Distance: 23 miles

Difficulty: Moderate to difficult

Blazes: Blue

Water: Generally plentiful; trail crosses many streams. First 7.5 miles of this section may have limited water in dry conditions.

Vegetation: Open hardwoods are most common; meadows; hemlocks primarily found along streams

Terrain: Level and rolling, with gradual changes in elevation. The beginning of this section has the steepest terrain.

Elevation change: 600 feet

Trail conditions: Generally well blazed and established, with a few brushy sections; often follows and crosses old forest roads and grades

Highlights: East and South Branches Tionesta Creek, Tionesta National Scenic Area, Tionesta Creek, scenic streams and campsites, boulders and rock outcrops

Directions:

Red Bridge: From the juncture of PA 59 and PA 321, at the Bradford Ranger Station, take PA 321 south 9.5 miles to a parking area on the right before the bridge. From Kane, take PA 321 9 miles north.

Longhouse Trailhead: From the juncture of PA 59 and PA 321, at the Bradford Ranger Station, take PA 321 south 11 miles to a large parking area on the left. From Kane, take PA 321 8 miles north. To reach the trail, cross PA 321 and hike up FR 262 to where the trail crosses.

US 6 (Ludlow): On the south side of US 6, there is a small parking area with sign, 1.7 miles east of Ludlow, 21 miles east of Warren, or 7.3 miles west of Kane.

PA 948: From the juncture of PA 948 and PA 66 near Chaffee, take PA 948 north for 5.4 miles and turn right on FR 148. Follow FR 148 for .3 mile to a parking area on the left. FR 148 is 3 miles south of Barnes along PA 948 and about 5 miles south of Sheffield.

Henrys Mills (PA 666): From the juncture of PA 666 and PA 948 at Barnes, take PA 666 west for 3.8 miles to Henrys Mills. After crossing the bridge, there is a pull-off parking area on the left.

This section explores the heart of the Tionesta region and features the Tionesta National Scenic and Research Areas, home to the largest old-growth forest between the Smoky Mountains and Adirondacks.

After crossing the bridge over the reservoir, follow PA 321 for approximately .1 mile. Turn right from the road and ascend gradually to the Longhouse Scenic Byway (FR 262). Cross that road and begin a steep 600-foot climb over .7 mile up the plateau, passing boulders and rock outcrops. At the top, the trail bears left onto an old forest road and reaches a vista over Kinzua Creek to the east. From the vista, the trail turns right and descends slightly to the edge of the plateau. Follow the level contour of the plateau's edge for .5 mile to the headwaters of a small stream. Pick up an old forest road and descend into the glen of another small stream. Begin a moderate climb to Gibbs Hill Road (T308); cross the road and ascend more steeply back to the top of the plateau. The trail levels and begins a gradual ascent for .2 mile before turning left along a private-property line. Descend 200 feet over .2 mile into the glen of a seasonal stream. The NCT makes a right turn, ascends back to the plateau along a road, and proceeds south in close proximity to a private-property line across rolling terrain for 1.5 miles. Descend to a small stream, turn left, and ascend gradually to the top of the plateau. A gradual 1.5-mile descent follows; cross a small stream and the trail drops 200 feet over .8 mile to US 6.

Cross US 6 where you find a trail sign and parking along the road. The NCT descends and crosses Twomile Run, ascends and crosses railroad tracks, and climbs more steeply before bearing right and crossing Wetmore Road. For the next mile, the trail crosses over the top of the plateau, passing gas wells, and intersects FR 133. Then it makes a .6-mile descent into a scenic glen with hemlocks along a small, babbling stream. Reach an area with several intersecting forest roads and cross a bridge over East Branch Tionesta Creek. The trail turns left and follows the scenic creek upstream under hemlocks, with nice campsites and a swimming hole. The NCT moves away from the creek and ascends the side of the plateau before descending into the valley of a small stream. Pass gas wells and cross forest roads as the trail gradually ascends the valley for approximately a mile. At the head of the valley, turn right and hike across rolling terrain, crossing three forestry roads and passing more gas wells. Reach the small parking area of the Tionesta National Scenic Area.

For the next .6 mile, the trail follows a circuitous route through the scenic area, with impressive views of the immense, ancient hemlock

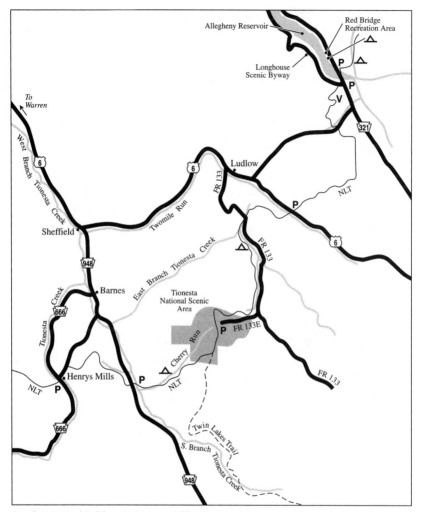

Section II: Red Bridge to Henrys Mills

trees. This is the premier highlight of this section. The forest was ravaged by a tornado, so it is somewhat open, with a lot of woody debris on the floor. Nevertheless, it is hard not to appreciate its beauty. Bear left onto a grassy pipeline swath with huge hemlocks growing from it. The gray/white-blazed scenic-area trail leaves to the left. Descend steeply along the swath to Cherry Run. Cross the run and climb 200 feet over .5 mile until the trail turns left, passes oil wells, and crosses a forest road. Turn right at a juncture with the Twin Lakes Trail.

The NCT crosses the forest road again and begins a 400-foot descent over a mile back toward Cherry Run. It reaches the scenic run, where there is potential camping, and follows it closely downstream for over a mile. Bear right onto a dirt forest road and follow it to a small parking area along South Branch Tionesta Creek with thick hemlocks. Cross a road bridge over the creek, turn from the road to the right, and ascend to PA 948.

Cross PA 948 and climb a short distance up the side of the mountain, until the trail turns right and gradually descends. Pass more oil wells and an access road. Turn left and ascend 300 feet over a mile along a small stream. At the top of the plateau are several old forest roads, and the trail turns left and passes still more wells. Hike across level terrain for .7 mile and cross a forest road; begin a slight descent and cross a pipeline swath. The trail descends more steeply along an old grade into the glen of a seasonal stream. Make a sharp left onto Henrys Mills Road and follow it for .5 mile as it descends to Henrys Mills. Bear right onto PA 666 and cross the bridge over Tionesta Creek.

Section III:
Henrys Mills to Kellettville

Duration: 2 to 3 days

Distance: 28.8 miles

Difficulty: Moderate

Blazes: Blue

Water: Generally plentiful

Vegetation: Open hardwoods with ferns; meadows; occasional groves of pines and hemlocks, with mountain laurel understory

Terrain: Level and rolling, with moderate changes in elevation

Elevation change: 400 feet

Trail conditions: Generally well blazed and established; a few brushy or boggy sections; trail often follows and crosses old forest roads and grades

Highlights: Minister Creek, massive boulders and outcrops, scenic streams and campsites, Tanbark Trail and Hearts Content National Scenic Area

Directions:

Henrys Mills (PA 666): From the juncture of PA 666 and PA 948 at Barnes, take PA 666 west for 3.8 miles to Henrys Mills. After crossing the bridge, there is a pull-off parking area on the left.

Dunham Siding: From Warren along US 6, get off at the Mohawk Avenue exit (there is a sign for Hearts Content Scenic Area), proceed south and bear right along Pleasant Drive (SR 3005), and follow for 11.5 miles. Bear left onto SR 2002 and follow for 3.7 miles to Hearts Content, on your left. From Tidioute, follow SR 3005 for 12 miles to SR 2002 and turn right. Heading south from Hearts Content and Hickory Creek Wilderness trailhead along SR 2002, proceed 2.1 miles farther, to FR 116 on your right. Follow this dirt forest road for .4 mile, until you reach a sign for the Tanbark and North Country Trail. There is parking along the road for two cars; a larger parking area for about five cars is just a short distance farther, on the right.

Kellettville: The best parking is at Kellettville Campground. From East Hickory, take PA 666 east for 10 miles to Kellettville, turn right, and cross the bridge to the campground. Park on the left side of the road. From Sheffield, take PA 666 west for 23.5 miles to Kellettville.

This section features the beautiful Minister Creek and massive rock outcrops. A worthwhile side trip along the Tanbark Trail will take you to the impressive old-growth forests at Hearts Content. Another advantage of this section is the convenient shuttle along PA 666.

After crossing the bridge, pass a pull-off parking area on the left and follow PA 666 for a few hundred yards. The trail makes a sharp right off the road at Messenger Run. Follow a grade as it gradually ascends the plateau above Tionesta Creek and away from Messenger Run. The NCT turns sharply to the left and gradually ascends around the flank of the plateau and into the glen of Messenger Run; the run is far below the trail. After a mile up the glen, the trail brings you closer to the small run. Cross a meadow, climb along the headwaters of the run, and cross over the top of the plateau. Begin a gradual descent followed by level hiking; after another mile, you reach Pell Run.

The NCT makes another sharp left turn away from the run and makes a mild climb back up the plateau along an old forest grade. Level terrain ensues for another mile, as the trail intersects grades and old forest roads. Turn left and descend 200 feet over .3 mile along a small stream to the scenic Upper Sheriff Run, with campsites. Cross the run and turn right as the trail gradually ascends the stream valley for over a mile along a grade that is at times above the run. Turn left and climb away from Upper Sheriff Run; this is a gentle climb that crosses a forest road at the top of the plateau. After you cross the road, level terrain follows for .6 mile before a 30-foot descent over .7 mile to scenic Lower Sheriff Run, with large rock outcrops, meadows, and

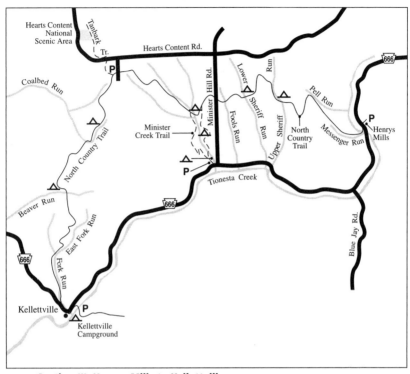

Section III: Henrys Mills to Kellettville

campsites. Cross the run and begin an immediate climb back up the plateau. Cross another forest road and make another descent along a small stream with large rock outcrops to Fools Run. Cross the run and follow it upstream for a short distance, until the trail climbs away from it and crosses Minister Hill Road (SR 2001).

After a slight ascent, the trail crosses level terrain and turns left to begin a gradual descent into a stream valley. Intersect the small stream and hike away from it to reach a juncture with the Minister Creek Trail; the NCT bears right. Follow level terrain with incredible boulders and rock outcrops. Descend gradually to Triple Fork Camp, an excellent camping area with streams and meadows. Make two stream crossings; after the second, the Minister Creek Trail leaves to the left while the NCT bears right and makes a gradual ascent up the stream valley along one of Minister Creek's branches. The Minister Creek Trail proceeds back to PA 666, featuring a crevasse, massive outcrops, and a beautiful vista along the way.

The NCT leads through hemlocks and past several springs. After a mile, it climbs gradually away from the stream and reaches a forest road. Bear right onto the road and follow it for .2 mile before turning left. Make a slight descent and hike along a grade across rolling terrain for almost 2 miles. There are many seep springs, and the trail can be boggy. Cross a small stream and reach FR 116 and the southern end of the Tanbark Trail. An excellent side trip is to follow the Tanbark Trail for approximately 2 miles to the beautiful old-growth forest of the Hearts Content National Scenic Area.

Cross FR 116 and a small parking area. Follow an old forest road for over a mile until the road turns into a grade. Turn left off the grade and ascend gradually up the valley of a small stream; cross the stream and continue the climb to the top of the plateau. Descend toward the headwaters of Coalbed Run and follow it downstream for a mile, with nice campsites. Turn left and leave the run to begin a 200-foot ascent over .5 mile. Descend to the source of another small stream, turn right, and intersect another forest road. Descend 300 feet over 1.4 miles along a tributary of Beaver Run. When you reach Beaver Run, with camping, cross the run and ascend to FR 449.

Cross FR 449 and descend into the valley. Pick up an old forest road and hike above East Fork. The trail turns right, ascends a drainage, and traverses rolling terrain along the edge of the plateau above East Fork. It then descends 200 feet over .5 mile to East Fork, where it crosses the stream. Turn right and follow East Fork downstream as it ascends the side of the plateau. Descend closer to the stream and the juncture of Middle and East Forks, where the stream becomes Fork Run. Follow the run downstream and cross an old forest road. The trail is often boggy along Fork Run. Continue to follow the run for a mile until the NCT ascends to the left and follows the contour of the plateau above the run for .6 mile. Descend gradually back to the run and cross a bridge. The trail then makes a short ascent to PA 666, on which it turns left. Follow PA 666 for approximately a mile and bear right onto a road that descends to and crosses Tionesta Creek. The Kellettville Campground is on the right.

Section IV:
Kellettville to Gravel Lick Road

Duration: 2 to 3 days

Distance: 31.8 miles

Difficulty: Easy to moderate

Blazes: Blue

Water: Generally plentiful

Vegetation: Open hardwoods with an understory of ferns; occasional pines, hemlocks, and meadows

Terrain: Level and rolling

Elevation change: 400 feet

Trail conditions: Generally well blazed and established; some sections brushy or boggy; often follows and crosses old forest roads and grades

Highlights: Rock outcrops, scenic streams, Amsler Springs, Cook Forest State Park, Forest Cathedral, old-growth forests, Seneca Point, Clarion River

Directions:

Kellettville: The best parking is at Kellettville Campground. From East Hickory, take PA 666 east for 10 miles to Kellettville, turn right, and cross the bridge to the campground. Park on the left side of the road. From Sheffield, take PA 666 west for 23.5 miles to Kellettville.

Amsler Springs: This is the southern trailhead in the Allegheny National Forest. From Kellettville Campground, follow FR 127 for a mile, and turn right onto FR 145. Follow this road for 7.3 miles, until you reach a parking area; a shelter and large camping area are nearby. From Marienville, take PA 66 south for 1.6 miles, turn right onto Muzette Road, and follow for 1.7 miles. Turn left onto FR 145 and follow for 1.2 miles to the trailhead.

Cook Forest State Park: From I-80, take Exit 78 and follow PA 36 north for 17 miles. PA 36 enters the park after crossing the Clarion River. There are two places in the state park that offers trailhead parking; if you intend to leave your car overnight, you must get permission from the state park first. To reach the Forest Cathedral, cross the Clarion River on PA 36 north and continue straight for .1 mile. Bear right onto SR 1015 and follow for .3 mile to a small pull-off parking area on both the left and right sides of the road. The NCT passes through this parking area. To reach the Log Cabin Inn parking area, cross the Clarion River on PA 36 north and continue straight for .1 mile. Bear right onto SR 1015 and follow for a mile to the Log Cabin Inn, Memorial Fountain, and parking area on the right. The NCT also passes through this parking area.

Contact information: Cook Forest State Park, PO Box 120, Cooksburg, PA
16217-0120; phone: 814-744-8407; e-mail: cookforestsp@state.pa.us;
website: www.dcnr.state.pa.us/stateparks/parks/cookforest.asp

---

This section features scenery similar to the previous. The premier
highlight is Cook Forest State Park, with beautiful streams, incredible
old-growth forests, views, and excellent hiking along the Clarion River.

Follow the road for 1.3 miles, until the trail leaves to the left. Hike
along a stream called the Branch for .2 mile. The trail turns right,
crosses FR 127, and ascends slightly before it levels along the plateau.
Begin a 200-foot ascent over .3 mile up the side of the plateau; the
trail, in typical fashion, levels off along the contour of the plateau and
traverses rolling terrain for almost a mile. This area was struck by the
May 1985 tornado. Turn right for a final gradual ascent between rock
outcrops to the top of the plateau and cross a forest road. Descend for
over a mile along a small stream to scenic Fourmile Run. Cross the run
and follow it downstream for .8 mile, until the trail climbs steeply to
the left. For the next .7 mile, follow the level contour of the plateau
above Salmon Creek.

The NCT becomes circuitous as it turns sharply to the right and
descends to a small stream. Cross the stream, turn left, and climb
along a grade out of the valley. Make another sharp turn to the right
and follow a level grade. Turn left and begin a short, gradual climb to
the top of a ridge, with views of Salmon Creek valley. Walk along the
ridge for .4 mile, turn right, and descend 250 feet along a small stream
to Guiton Run. Follow the run downstream for a short distance, cross
it, and climb out of the valley along a gradual grade. The NCT turns
right and descends steeply along another small, seasonal stream. Turn
left and follow the scenic Little Salmon Creek upstream for .4 mile,
with boggy terrain. Turn right and cross a bridge over the creek, with
good campsites.

Begin a steep ascent and climb along switchbacks until the trail levels off and ascends gradually up a small stream valley. Turn right and
make a semicircle before the trail turns left and climbs to the top of a
ridge with large rock outcrops. The trail descends gradually from the
ridge and levels before crossing a pipeline swath. Ascend slightly and
begin a 400-foot descent over a mile to FR 145. Bear right on the road
and follow it across Salmon Creek and a small parking area. Turn right

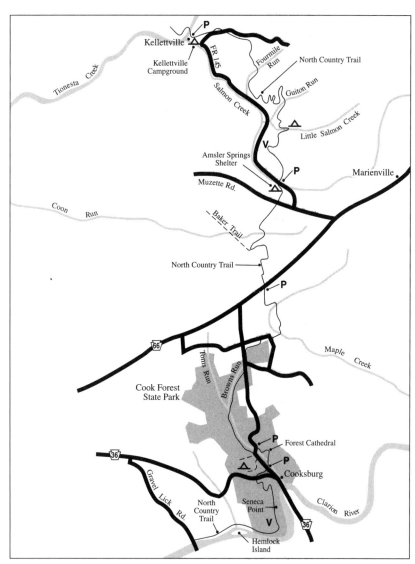

Section IV: Kellettville to Gravel Lick Road

off the road and pass Amsler Springs Shelter in a large meadow. Hike gradually along a small stream with hemlocks for .5 mile and turn right to climb out of the valley. The trail levels at the top and crosses the paved Muzette Road (SR 3004).

Cross the road and descend to another forest road, which the trail crosses. Descend into the shallow valley of a tributary of Coon Run, with hemlocks. Turn left and descend to Coon Run. Cross a bridge over the run; wetlands and ponds lie downstream. Gradually ascend for .7 mile to the plateau; the trail leaves the national forest and enters state game lands. Reach a juncture with the Baker Trail to the right. From here to Gravel Lick Road, the NCT and Baker Trail follow the same route. The Baker Trail is a 141-mile backpacking trail that begins near Freeport and ends a mile north of this juncture.

Make two quick lefts and follow a forest road for .8 mile. Turn right onto another forest road and follow for .3 mile; the trail turns left. Ascend slightly and then descend to a small stream. Cross the stream and ascend gradually to the plateau. Cross railroad tracks and, soon thereafter, PA 66. Descend for .6 mile and bear left, until the trail crosses the scenic Maple Creek. Ascend gradually for .7 mile and cross Maple Creek Road before the NCT descends and crosses Maple Creek again. Climb to and turn right on Jacks Hollow Road, and then turn left onto Maple Creek Road. Follow this road for .2 mile before turning left; the NCT enters Cook Forest State Park.

Cook Forest is one of Pennsylvania's premier state parks. The NCT travels the length of the park, offering many scenic features. This last segment of trail is a true joy to hike. Wilderness camping is not permitted in the park, but a side trail leads to the campground, only .4 mile from the NCT.

Upon entering the park, the trail turns right along the park boundary. Off to the left is an old-growth forest. After .5 mile, the trail bends right and descends slightly. Cross Greenwood Road and then SR 1015. Descend along the headwaters of Browns Run and follow the run for 1.5 miles. The trail turns left and crosses a bridge over the run. Turn right and continue along Browns Run as it ripples down a smaller, scenic glen with boulders and cascades. The trail turns right onto Toms Run Road and follows it for a short distance, then turns left off the road. Cross a bridge over Toms Run and follow a grade to the left above the run. After .4 mile, pass a bridge and trail to the left and a cascading water slide. Continue to follow the grade above the run and cross bridges over two small side streams. Beautiful hemlocks often grow along the trail. Corduroy Trail joins from the right, and .3 mile farther, Camp Trail joins from the right. Follow this trail to the campground if you need a place to camp. Camping here requires a fee.

Reach SR 1015 and follow the road a short distance to the left. Reach the Log Cabin Inn, with interpretive displays, picnic facilities, restrooms, water, and parking area. Hike up to Memorial Fountain and follow the grade into the spectacular Forest Cathedral, with its majestic old-growth pines and web of trails. Climb 150 feet over .2 mile along a drainage, and then descend gradually through this remarkable forest. The size of the trees and serenity of this forest are inspiring. Cross a bridge over Toms Run and climb up to a small parking area and SR 1015. Cross the road and follow the Hemlock Trail up a glen shaded with handsome, old-growth hemlocks. At times the climb is somewhat steep; the trail bears left and crosses PA 36 at a curve, so be careful crossing. Continue to climb through a beautiful ancient hemlock forest. The trail levels as it meanders through the forest before descending between ledges and rock outcrops and passing through small meadows. As it climbs back to the plateau, the trail continues to meander. Follow the rim through a lovely hemlock and pine forest.

Pass Mohawk and Seneca Trails; the NCT tunnels through rhododendrons between rock ledges. Pass behind a parking area and restrooms, and then ascend to a side trail to the right that leads to Seneca Point. This vista offers an incredible view from cliffs of the Clarion River and its twisting valley. Return to the NCT and pass the fire tower, which you can climb for more views. Boulders and ledges surround the tower. Begin a steep, 350-foot descent over .6 mile; do not cut across the many switchbacks. Notice the forest has changed to hardwoods with a thick understory of mountain laurel.

Reach the Clarion River, with hemlocks and rhododendrons. Side trails lead down to the bank, where you are treated to views of the river and its scenic gorge. The scenery is unspoiled by development, and this section of the river is not nearly as crowded with canoeists, who usually take out at Cooksburg. The trail stays within view of the river and moves even closer to it. Pass the River Trail to the right and enter State Game Lands 283. The trail continues along the river, crossing the scenic Henry Run and offering views of Hemlock Island in the river. Pick up an old grade and follow it along the Clarion for almost a mile. This section ends at Gravel Lick Road, where there is no space for parking. The Baker Trail turns left, crosses the bridge, and continues south along Cathers Run. There is some space for pull-off parking along the road across the river.

62. Twin Lakes Trail

Duration: 1 1/2 to 2 days

Distance: 16.5-mile linear trail

Difficulty: Easy to moderate

Blazes: White/gray diamonds

Water: Generally plentiful

Vegetation: Northern hardwoods predominant, with a thick understory of ferns; hemlocks and pines common along streams; open meadows; wetlands

Terrain: Mostly level or rolling, with gradual changes in elevation; numerous stream crossings

Elevation change: 600 feet

Trail conditions: Generally well blazed, often following old grades and forest roads; sections unestablished and brushy or wet and boggy; some stream crossings without bridges (the one over South Branch Tionesta Creek has failed)

Highlights: Scenic streams and woodlands, backcountry fishing, good camping, wildlife, beaver dams

Directions:

Twin Lakes Campground: From Kane, drive 6.1 miles south on PA 321. Turn right and follow FR 191 2 miles to the campground area. The trail begins a few hundred feet along a gated road, straight ahead from the entrance road. From Wilcox, proceed north for 3 miles along PA 321.

PA 66: From Kane, follow PA 66 south for 4.6 miles, to the trail crossing with a sign. Some parking is available along a forest road that joins from the left before the trail crossing. From the juncture of PA 948 and PA 66, proceed north on PA 66 toward Kane for almost 3 miles to the trail crossing.

Western End: The western end of the trail does not have an established trailhead; it is best reached by FR 443. From the juncture of PA 948 and PA 66 near Chaffee, proceed north on PA 948 for 3.7 miles to Brookston. Turn right onto Fork Run Road; continue straight onto Beanfarm Road and proceed 1.5 miles as the road ascends and passes the trail, marked by an Overlook sign. Continue farther a short distance, until the road makes a sharp left; you'll find a place to park on the right. This road can be gated and may be impassable in winter. Brookston is located 7 miles south of Sheffield along PA 948.

Contact information: Allegheny National Forest, PO Box 847, Warren, PA 16365; phone: 814-723-5150; websites: www.fs.fed.us/r9/forests/allegheny, www.allegheny-online.com/hikingtrails.html

The Twin Lakes Trail (TLT) is a linear trail that connects the Twin Lakes Recreation Area to the North Country Trail in the Tionesta Scenic Area. The Twin Lakes Recreation Area is a modern campground with electrical hookups, showers, restrooms, and picnic area; you can camp here for a fee.

This trail passes and explores a variety of streams and often crosses wet or boggy terrain. Wolf Run, East Branch Tionesta Creek, and Crane Run are good freestone trout streams. Crane Run has been designated a wilderness trout stream by the Pennsylvania Fish and Boat Commission. These attributes make the trail ideal for backcountry fly fishing.

The section of forest through which this trail passes has many oil and gas wells, so expect to see access roads, pipes, pumps, and other machinery along the trail. Maintenance along the trail has been problematic because of storm damage, and the bridge over South Branch Tionesta Creek has failed. The Twin Lakes Trail is not as popular as others in the national forest, so you can enjoy a lot of isolation.

To reach the beginning of the TLT from the recreation area, you must first hike a .7-mile section along the Black Cherry Interpretive Trail; the TLT leaves from the far end of this trail's half loop. Make a gradual ascent until the trail levels off at the top of the plateau. The trail follows an old forest road and crosses FR 331 at a telephone swath. In another .3 mile, cross FR 331 again. After a slight descent, the trail levels and crosses FR 138, with some parking. You will then pass a juncture with the Mill Creek Trail to your left; this linear trail proceeds south to PA 948 and the Brush Hollow trail system.

After more level hiking for almost .6 mile, cross SR 4009 and begin a gradual descent into the upper valley of Wolf Run. The trail goes down to the stream over the course of a mile, often following an old railroad grade across boggy terrain. Follow the run downstream to your left, cross a footbridge with hemlocks, and gradually ascend the side of the plateau. Begin a mild descent to PA 66, with parking along the road, and cross a small stream. The TLT once again traverses the side of the plateau and enters a small glen. The trail mildly ascends the plateau before a long, gradual descent to Coon Run. It then follows the run along an old grade for almost a mile across boggy terrain and past beaver dams and hemlocks. Here you'll find potential camping. The TLT climbs gradually away from Coon Run, crosses FR 152 and a small parking area, and descends 200 feet over .5 mile to Wolf Run.

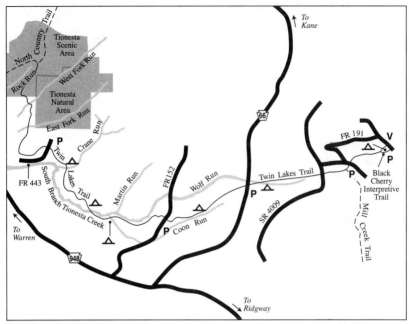

Hike 62: Twin Lakes Trail

Bear left near the run and proceed downstream along a grade; the trail is rarely in sight of the run and stays on the side of the bank. After 1.4 mile, the trail mildly descends and crosses Coon Run. Nice camping is available in this area.

Follow South Branch Tionesta Creek downstream for roughly a mile, across wet terrain and past more beaver activity. Cross the creek itself, as the bridge has failed, and ascend gradually away from the run. The TLT levels off, wraps around the side of the plateau, and drops gradually to the scenic Crane Run with hemlocks, pines, and potential campsites. Here the trail enters its western end, where there are greater variations in elevation. This section of the trail is more challenging, but the terrain can be handled easily by the beginner. Cross Crane Run and make a long, gradual ascent until the trail crosses a small stream after a mile.

You will now begin a steeper climb to the plateau, covering 200 feet over .3 mile. At the top, maintain your elevation along the edge of the plateau until you begin a long, gradual descent around its flank. Cross East Fork Run, where another moderate climb awaits you, this one covering almost 300 feet over .5 mile. Now begin an 180-foot descent over .4 mile to West Fork Run. Cross the run and begin the longest and most difficult ascent of the trail, a climb covering almost 300 feet over .5 mile. At the top, level hiking returns as the trail enters the Tionesta Scenic Area. The TLT ends at its juncture with the North Country Trail.

63. Hickory Creek Trail

Duration: 1 to 2 days

Distance: 12-mile loop

Difficulty: Easy to moderate

Blazes: Yellow blazes are faded and not maintained, but trail is clearly established

Water: Generally plentiful

Vegetation: Northern hardwood forest predominant, with occasional hemlocks and white pines; some trees sizable; glades and meadows common along streams; understory dominated by ferns

Terrain: Trail follows mostly level or rolling terrain, with gradual changes in elevation

Elevation change: 300 feet

Trail conditions: Well established and maintained, but most blazes faded; no bridges across streams; some blowdowns

Highlights: Hickory Creek Wilderness is a congressionally designated wilderness area, with scenic streams and campsites, woodlands, meadows and glades, wildlife

Directions:

Hearts Content Scenic Area and Hickory Creek Wilderness trailhead: From Warren along US 6, get off at the Mohawk Avenue exit (there is a sign for Hearts Content Scenic Area), proceed south and bear right along Pleasant Drive (SR 3005), and follow for 11.5 miles. Bear left onto SR 2002 and follow for 3.7 miles to Hearts Content, on your left. From Tidioute, follow SR 3005 for 12 miles to SR 2002 and turn right. (Note: The ANF may build a new trailhead for this trail along SR 2002, just north of the present one.)

Contact information: Allegheny National Forest, PO Box 847, Warren, PA 16365; phone: 814-723-5150; websites: www.fs.fed.us/r9/forests/allegheny and www.allegheny-online.com/hikingtrails.html

The Hickory Creek Trail (HCT) traverses the Hickory Creek Wilderness, one of two such wilderness areas in the national forest, along with the Allegheny Islands Wilderness Area. These special areas are free from the forest roads, logging, oil wells, ATV and snowmobile trails, and gas lines that exist on much of the Allegheny National Forest. The serenity of Hickory Creek is something to relish, as are its scenic woodlands, which will only grow more beautiful as the trees mature. The HCT is an easy and popular trail that can be day-hiked. This is a great trail for younger or beginning backpackers. This description follows the loop clockwise.

The trail leaves the Hearts Content Picnic Area through a symmetrical plantation of red pines. Bear left, cross SR 2002, and walk under utility lines. The HCT passes a register and reaches the beginning of the loop, which is about .5 mile from Hearts Content. Turn left and gradually descend along a grade through hardwoods and several deep groves of hemlocks. After .8 mile from the register, the trail leaves the grade to the left and crosses a small stream. There are campsites downstream to the left off the trail. Continue to follow an old grade along the contour of the plateau for .7 mile. Make a short climb to the

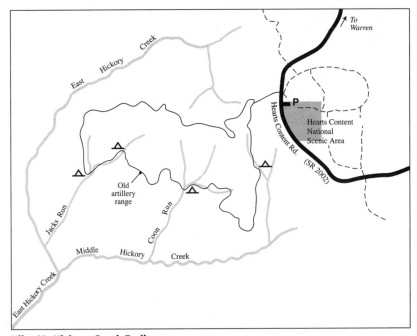

Hike 63: Hickory Creek Trail

top of the plateau and follow level terrain for .5 mile before descending into the drainage of Coon Run.

Cross a seasonal side stream and follow the side of the plateau above the stream. Descend 150 feet over .5 mile and cross the stream; off to your right are large meadows. Hike downstream, passing nice campsites. The trail bends right, crosses Coon Run, passes through a meadow, and reenters the forest. Begin a gradual 100-foot climb over .5 mile back to the plateau. After the climb, the trail levels off and cuts through a long meadow that was once an artillery range, then begins a long, gradual, .8-mile descent to the scenic Jacks Run.

Cross Jacks Run at a campsite and proceed downstream along an old grade through extensive meadows with hemlocks and pines. Follow Jacks Run for about .5 mile, with some of the nicest scenery along the trail. When you reach a large meadow and campsites, turn right to begin another ascent to the plateau. The old grade proceeds straight through the meadow and heads downstream. The climb is gradual, rising 200 feet over .7 mile. At the edge of the plateau, the trail descends and follows rolling sidehill along the contour of the plateau. After about .5 mile, the trail ascends back to the top. Continue a moderate climb until the trail bends right and passes large boulders and outcrops.

For the next .5 mile, the terrain is level and rolling, before the trail climbs over a small hill. Hike above the drainage into East Hickory Creek underneath a mixture of hemlocks, pines, and hardwoods. Cross an old grade and make a sharp left. After .25 mile, the trail bends right and passes an established side trail that descends to East Hickory Creek. Hike along the edge of a steep slope above the East Hickory Creek drainage to your left. The trail mildly ascends and returns to the beginning of the loop. There are no established campsites along the northern half of the trail from Jacks Run.

🥾 64. Tanbark Trail

Duration: 1 to 2 days

Distance: 9-mile linear trail

Difficulty: Easy to moderate

Blazes: White/gray diamond blazes

Water: Generally plentiful

Vegetation: Northern hardwood forest with thick understory of ferns; mountain laurel; groves of hemlocks and pines; open meadows and glades

Terrain: Rolling or level along the top of the plateau; ascents and descents reaching 200 vertical feet where the trail crosses stream valleys and glens; most difficult terrain at the northern end, where the trail climbs or drops 800 feet over 2 miles, with the section closest to US 62 being particularly steep

Elevation change: 800 feet

Trail conditions: Well blazed and established

Highlights: Impressive boulders, rock outcrops, and other formations; scenic streams with cascades; hemlock forests

Directions:

Southern trailhead (FR 116): Heading south from Hearts Content and Hickory Creek Wilderness trailhead along SR 2002, proceed 2.1 miles farther until you reach FR 116 to your right. Follow this dirt forest road for .4 mile until you reach a sign for the Tanbark and North Country Trail. There is parking along the road for two cars; a larger parking area for about five cars is just a short distance farther, on the right.

Hearts Content Scenic Area and Hickory Creek Wilderness trailhead: The Tanbark Trail can also be conveniently accessed from this trailhead. From Warren along US 6, get off at the Mohawk Avenue exit (there is a sign for Hearts Content Scenic Area), proceed south and bear right along Pleasant Drive (SR 3005), and follow for 11.5 miles. Bear left onto SR 2002 and follow for 3.7 miles to Hearts Content, on your left. From Tidioute, follow SR 3005 for 12 miles to SR 2002 and turn right.

Northern trailhead (US 62): From the Warren area, proceed south on US 62 from US 6 for 7.2 miles. Look for a small trailhead sign and parking along the road. This trailhead is also located 9 miles north of Tidioute along US 62.

Contact information: Allegheny National Forest, PO Box 847, Warren, PA 16365; phone: 814-723-5150; websites: www.fs.fed.us/r9/forests/allegheny and www.allegheny-online.com/hikingtrails.html

The Tanbark Trail (TT) is a short, linear trail that can be day-hiked if you shuttle cars or backpacked for a pleasant 2-day, 1-night trip. It can also be part of an extended trip accessing Hickory Creek Wilderness, the North Country Trail, or Minister Creek. The TT's southern end is at its juncture with the North Country Trail; it passes near the Hearts Content Scenic Area and proceeds northwest to US 62, where the northern trailhead can be found. This trail's finest features are massive boulders and rock outcrops in its northern section. Another highlight is the scenic glen carved by Boardinghouse Run, with moss-covered boulders, cascades, and hemlocks.

From its southern end at its juncture with the North Country Trail and FR 116, the TT proceeds west along level terrain through a hardwood forest. Cross FR 119 and follow the trail as it turns right (north) along rolling terrain. Enter a scenic hemlock forest and cross the headwaters of Middle Hickory Creek. The trail climbs gradually and crosses Hearts Content Road (SR 2002).

The forest changes back to stately hardwoods, with an understory of ferns and interspersed hemlocks and pines. The terrain is level, and the trail bends to the left and passes a juncture with the Ironwood Loop to the right. Proceed on the TT as it follows the western half of the Ironwood Loop; here the trail has both gray/white and blue blazes. Hemlocks become more common as the trail makes a short climb to the top of the plateau. For the next .3 mile, the terrain is level as the trail meanders through a diverse forest of hemlocks, pines and hardwoods, and small meadows. Blowdowns may be common along this section.

The trail descends from the plateau through a hardwood forest until it reaches the scenic West Branch Tionesta Creek, with a nice campsite under hemlock and pine trees. A blue-blazed trail proceeds down the stream; follow the gray/white blazes. Gradually climb away from the creek along the outskirts of the Hearts Content Scenic Area. The forest is beautiful, with large hemlocks and beeches. When you reach the blue-blazed Tom's Run Loop, turn left and follow this trail for a short distance, until the TT leaves to the right and gradually climbs up the plateau. Cross the level top for .2 mile, then descend more steeply into a hemlock forest and reach the blue-blazed Toms Run Loop again, where the TT follows to the left.

Follow the loop for .1 mile through a verdant forest, until the TT leaves to the right and crosses Tom Run. Soon thereafter, it crosses Hearts Content Road (SR 2002), where there is a pull-off area for park-

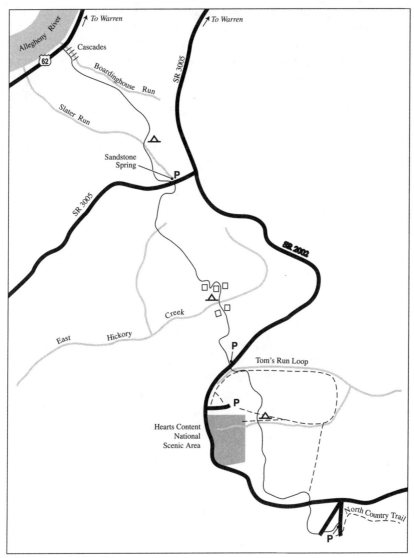

Hike 64: Tanbark Trail

ing. The trail follows a slight ascent for .2 mile, then descends and turns right along the contour of the plateau. Make a sharp left as the trail descends steeply through a crevasse between rock outcrops. After leaving the crevasse, pass a large boulder with hemlocks growing from the top to your left. The trail descends into this scenic forested valley and crosses a bridge over the lovely East Hickory Creek. The forest is dominated by thick hemlocks. Campsites are off to your left.

As the trail climbs gradually from the creek, the forest changes dramatically to hardwoods and mountain laurel. Pass large boulders off to your right. Soon the trail passes in front of a monstrous overhanging ledge and huge boulders. This is an excellent spot to take a rest. The trail climbs above the outcrops and follows the rim of the plateau for .5 mile. Rolling terrain follows for .4 mile, then the trail makes a short descent into a glen carved by a small stream. Begin a long, gradual ascent for .3 mile from the small stream to a ridge; thereafter, the trail descends to Sandstone Spring and US 337.

Cross US 337 and pass a parking area to the right that used to be a picnic area. The trail traverses level terrain through a hardwood forest with mountain laurel. Cross small seasonal streams and begin a gradual descent through thick laurel along Slater Run. Cross a bridge over Slater Run and pass scenic campsites. Begin a gradual, 160-foot climb along an old grade up to the plateau. At the top, the trail bears left and leaves the grade; begin a slight descent and merge left onto another old grade.

Hemlocks and pines become more common, as the TT descends gradually into Boardinghouse Run's glen. The run moves out of sight as the descent steepens, with boulders, outcrops, and hemlocks. The run cascades below the trail; its streambed is filled with moss-covered boulders. The trail becomes very steep as it descends into the glen and rejoins Boardinghouse Run, with scenic cascades and small waterfalls. Cross a utility line and hike down to US 62, with parking across the road.

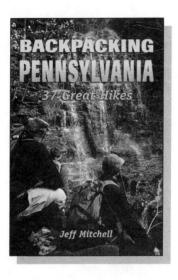

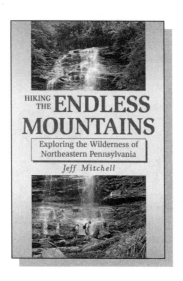